12 SIMPLE SECRETS

of HAPPINESS

in a

TOPSY-TURVY WORLD

—

Glenn Van Ekeren

Prentice
Hall Press

Library of Congress Cataloging-in-Publication Data

Van Ekeren, Glenn.
  12 simple secrets of happiness in a topsy-turvy world / by Glenn Van Ekeren.
  p. cm.
  ISBN 0-7352-0362-8
  1. Happiness.   2. Conduct of life.   I. Title: Twelve simple secrets of happiness
in a topsy-turvy world.   II. Title.

BJ1481 .V36 2002
158.1—dc21   2001058793

Acquisitions Editor: Tom Power
Senior Production Editor: Jackie Roulette
Composition: Robyn Beckerman
Design: Sue Behnke

©2002 by Glenn Van Ekeren

Printed in the United States of America

10 9 8 7 6 5 4 3 2 1

ISBN 0-7352-0362-8

ATTENTION: CORPORATIONS AND SCHOOLS

Prentice Hall Press books are available at quantity discounts with bulk purchase for educational, business, or sales promotional use. For information, please write to: Prentice Hall Special Sales, 240 Frisch Court, Paramus, New Jersey 07652. Please supply: title of book, ISBN, quantity, how the book will be used, date needed.

 Paramus, NJ 07652

http://www.phpress.com

CONTENTS

ACKNOWLEDGMENTS

This book is dedicated to my father, Delmar Van Ekeren, and my father-in-law, Jon McClure, who fought courageous battles with cancer. They loved life with a passion and—although the cancer took their lives—their legacy lives on in spirit and in memory.

INTRODUCTION

We live in a stressful world. Today is not guaranteed to be a repeat of yesterday and the future isn't what it used to be. Times are quickly changing. The pace of life is rapidly increasing. People are caught in the middle of a whirlwind of change waiting for the "good old days" to return, but it has no intention of making a comeback.

Wouldn't it be great if we could eliminate the stress, pressure, and problems of life. Surprise! It wouldn't be great at all. We would achieve very little, there would be no challenges to help us grow, and life would get boring. Stress, adversity, obstacles, and change are natural and oftentimes desirable bits of life. The best way to survive and thrive today is to create the life we want despite the circumstances that surround us.

Each selection in this book is designed to help you take charge of your life. The real-life stories, powerful quotes, doses of humor, and inspirational applications will encourage you to excel in every area of your life. You'll discover time-less wisdom to provide you with up-to-date insights for achieving greater levels of success in your life. You will feel empowered to make a difference in how your day and life work out.

Feeling burned out, used up, overloaded, or just plain worn out isn't necessary. You can make the best of today's changing world, learn to capitalize on the opportunities change produces, and create a brighter future. Learn to antic-ipate, accept, adapt—even embrace—the challenges of change. Discover the skills and attitudes necessary to deal with the daily ups and downs. Take charge of your actions and reactions as well as the situations that presently hinder your ability to enjoy life in the fast lane.

I hope you'll be encouraged, motivated, and challenged as you read each selection. Dwell on one a day or devour the entire book in one sitting. Either way, you are bound to gain unshakable confidence and determination to make your life just a little bit better today than it was yesterday.

12 SIMPLE SECRETS

of HAPPINESS *in a*

TOPSY-TURVY WORLD

LIVE LIFE TO THE FULLEST

The word 'now' plays a big part in my life. I'm not particularly interested in the ten-year plan. I want to know, what am I doing today? Is this a good day? And amazingly, most of them are good days.

LINDA ELLERBEE

LIVE IN THE "NOW"

Garfield and his owner Jon were pictured in one of their typical cartoon conversations. Jon is in one of his philosophical moods as he questions whether or not he has lived any former lives.

Garfield throws Jon one of his "you've got to be kidding" looks as he seriously doubts the prospect of Jon's reincarnation because, "You're not even living this life."

Jon's not alone. Some people are so preoccupied with "former" lives or the anticipation of "future" lives that they completely overlook this life. They become obsessed with "what could have been" or "what might be" that they are oblivious to "what is."

I'm well aware of how beneficial it can be to learn from the past and build on it. I'm also an avid believer in living within a future vision I choose for my life. In fact, I'm never happier than when I'm pursuing my dreams for a better life. I'm energized knowing exactly the direction I want

You don't have to be intelligent, good-looking, or rich to get what you want out of life. There are lots and lots of situations which you can use as an excuse to win or as an excuse to fail. Choosing to be responsible for your life puts you in control over it.

W. MITCHELL

my life to go. But, I'm living fully in the moment to make those aspirations a reality.

I've experienced firsthand what happens to people so imprisoned by their past that today could hardly be characterized as living. I encountered lives that were driven by survival when I worked as a jail administrator. People in the normal world get caught in ruts, but in the penal system, the rut becomes a grave. Ellen Glasgow said, "The only difference between a rut and a grave is their dimensions." Many of the people I worked with had dug themselves a very small hole that suffocated hope from their lives.

Prisoners rarely take advantage of the structured system to put their past behind them and work to improve the quality of their lives. Once they are sentenced by the courts, a severely restricted mindset dominates their life. Freedom is gone. Personal dignity is diminished. The activities of their day are dictated to them. Personal identity is replaced with jail uniforms. This is not living—it's existing. And, once in the system, few choose to escape their self-made grave even when the sentence is fulfilled.

I also spent several years working with juvenile delinquent youth. The difference between this population and people who had been in the prison system for a long time is that I always believed there was a ray of hope for these young people. Maybe they were not yet indoctrinated into an irresponsible lifestyle. The goal was always to help them live each day within acceptable guidelines and create an internal desire to keep the hope for a better life alive. This might sound like a reasonable task, but you would be amazed how many young people were firmly connected and comfortable with failure. It was a difficult task to help them change the image they possessed of themselves so they could begin believing a better life was possible.

I came away from these professional experiences with the convictions that:

1. The earlier in life we connect people to the value of life, the better our chances for helping them live in the "now."

2. Once we fall into the rut of refusing to take responsibility for our lives, there is little hope for improving the quality of our lives.

3. People who live in a literal, mental, or emotional prison rarely accept responsibility for their current condition.

4. Those who want to do, what they want to do, when they want to do it, often end up in places where people tell them what to do, when, and how to do it, and whether or not they'll ever get to do what they want to do again.

5. Unless people view themselves as valuable, as lovable, and respectable, they will rarely develop a positive view of life.

The only way to live in the "now" is to accept each minute of every day as an unrepeatable precious moment. It is a valuable gift for which we have the responsibility to take ownership. Love your work. Enjoy your play. Laugh often. Cherish the good times. Shed your tears in the sad times. Believe that whatever happens today is preparation for the challenges, opportunities, and possibilities you'll encounter tomorrow.

LOOSEN YOUR GRIP

I was fortunate enough as a high school junior to land a job at an all-new automatic car wash. It was a high-tech operation featuring rotating soft brushes, rollers that automatically forwarded the vehicle, and a high-powered dryer. (If this doesn't sound too high tech, remember the year was 1969.)

When I grip the wheel too tight, I find I lose control.

STEVE RAPSON

Customers loved the end result but many struggled with the automation. "Please make sure all windows are up, drive your car forward until the stoplight flashes, put your car in neutral, and let the machine do the rest" were the instructions I gave to every customer.

Everything went as planned until the conveyor began pushing the car forward and a sudden rush of soap and water blinded people's vision. Customers would frequently hit their brakes, frantically honk their horn, and even attempt to steer their car, often causing the tires to become jammed against the guide rails.

I can't count the number of times I would be forced to turn off the machine, navigate my way through dripping soap and water to the driver, and remind him or her to relax and let the machine do the work. Soon the car would be propelled into the outside world—washed, polished, and dried.

It was amazing how many times people would return the next week and repeat their blunders. Some people adjusted quickly to giving up control of the car, but the majority found it difficult to trust a machine. Ironically, the more they tried to control the situation, the more disastrous the outcome.

Although I never had difficulty in a car wash, I've encountered similar emotions during life situations. When I feel confident and in control, things seem to go quite smoothly. However, when my energies are directed at events beyond my control, I get frustrated, panic, and want to apply the brakes or steer my way clear of the struggle.

There are times in all of our lives when we've followed the instructions, prepared ourselves the best we can, and have aligned our thoughts, attitudes, and feelings with the demands of the situation. We're in control. But there are other factors including other people, extenuating circumstances, or unex-

pected obstacles that thunderously appear. Suddenly we realize the best laid plans aren't good enough. Relax.

Sometimes, all you can do is all you can do. Put the situation in perspective, focus on those things you have some
ability to control, and loosen your grip on the steering
wheel. You may be surprised how polished you come out the
other side.

*I like living. I
have sometimes
been wildly,
despairingly,
acutely miser-
able, racked
with sorrow,
but through it
all I still know
quite certainly
that just to
be alive is a
grand thing.*

AGATHA
CHRISTIE

HOLD TIGHT TO
YOUR PURPOSE

*Nothing
contributes so
much to
tranquilize the
mind as
a steady
purpose—a
point on which
the soul
may fix its
intellectual
eye.*

MARY
SHELLEY

It doesn't take a futurist, prophet, or fortuneteller to predict your future. I can do it for you. Answer this question: What is your purpose in life and what plans have you made to attain it?

You wouldn't believe the varied answers I've received to that question. Some people simply want to exist; others want lots of money and success; still others get almost mystical about it. Don't make this philosophical. What do you want out of life? What is your supreme aim? What do you have a burning desire to be and achieve? The question that puts it all in perspective for me is this: What drives your life?

Harold Kushner wrote, "Our souls are not hungry for fame, comfort, wealth, or power. Those rewards create almost as many problems as they solve. Our souls are hungry for meaning, for the sense that we have figured out how to live so that our lives matter, so that the world will at least be a little bit different for our having passed through it."

Mother Teresa was a marvelous example of Kushner's advice. She didn't necessarily set out for a career helping the poor. In fact, she taught the wealthiest children of Calcutta, India for 20 years. Living in the wealthy neighborhood overlooking the impoverished slums kept her contained in comfort.

Walking down the streets below one night, she heard a woman crying out for help. As this dying woman fell into Mother Teresa's arms, her life changed forever. Her purpose was discovered.

She rushed the woman to the hospital and was told to sit and wait. Knowing the woman was in dire need of medical assistance, she took her to another hospital where she was also told she would have to wait. Mother Teresa realized the woman was being denied medical attention because of her social status, so she took the woman home where she later died in Mother Teresa's arms.

It was then that this woman of extraordinary courage and compassion pledged this would never happen again. She dedicated her life to easing the pain of the suffering and pursued a purpose that whether suffering people lived or died, they would do so with dignity. Countless numbers of people have been treated with love and respect like never before because of Mother Teresa.

I doubt Mother Teresa ever got up in the morning and said: "What another lousy day in the changing streets of Calcutta." No way. Every minute of every day of her life was driven by a specific purpose.

Purpose gives us a meaningful and fulfilling reason for living. It keeps us attentive to our life's priorities and increases our tolerance for ambiguity. A compelling purpose provides the motivation for us to do the things we don't like to do, but need to do in order to move us closer to our purpose. Flexibility increases as a renewed positive anticipation of the future emerges. That's the power of purposeful living.

Purpose allows you to keep change in perspective. Those who possess a strong sense of purpose and commitment, who consistently view change as a challenge to master instead of a threat, aren't overwhelmed by the stress of change.

James Allen probably said it best: "They who have no central purpose in life fall easy prey to petty worries, fears, troubles, and self-pitying, all of which lead to failure, unhappiness, and loss . . . for weakness cannot persist in a power evolving universe." If all you do is react to change based on your emotions, survival will become your primary goal. Purpose provides the direction for you to make sense out of the irrational and sometimes unpredictable world in which you live.

The challenge is not to create a purpose, but to *discover* the purpose that already exists within you. Holding tight to your purpose will produce fullness of life in spite of the multitude of events attempting to manipulate you. "There's no grander sight in the world," believed Orison Swett Marden, "than that of a person fired with a great purpose, dominated by one unwavering aim."

Successful people have a strong purpose. Strong enough to make them form the habit of doing things they don't like to do in order to accomplish the purpose they want to accomplish.

EARL NIGHTINGALE

LOOSEN UP! LIGHTEN UP!
LIVE IT UP!

Humor is the great thing, the saving thing. The minute it crops up, all our irritations and resentments slip away, and a sunny spirit takes their place.

MARK
TWAIN

❀

I f you want to increase the quality of your life, listen carefully: Develop your sense of humor. Roger Ailes wrote in a *Success* magazine article entitled, "Lighten Up: Stuffed Shirts Have Short Careers," "The only advice some of my clients need when they come to see me can be summed up in two words: Lighten up. It's ironic, but your career can depend on whether you get serious about taking yourself less seriously."

Our tendency toward a seriously stuffy, sanctimonious, sophistication toward life needs a healthy injection of infectious humor.

A poll conducted by *Entertainment Weekly* magazine found that 82 percent of the people who go to movies want to laugh, 7 percent want to cry, and 3 percent want to scream. I definitely fall into the 82-percent bracket. When I go to the movies, I normally scout out the comedies. Science fiction gives me a headache. Suspense makes my stomach tense. Dramas are just too depressing. But laughter-producing comedies stimulate my immune system. Besides, when I'm laughing, I can put the cares of the world aside because it is virtually impossible to think of anything else.

I received a call from my brother around supper time on a Friday evening. It was a call I anxiously awaited. My dad hadn't been feeling well and his doctor was running a series of tests. His iron was low, but in addition, the doctor was uncomfortable with the lumps he felt in the abdomen area.

The call confirmed my greatest fear. "I have bad news, Glenn," Joel said. "Dad has cancer." There was an uncomfortable silence and then I asked, "When do you want me there?" It was decided I would come the next morning to be with Dad as he underwent a series of tests to confirm the doctor's suspicions and determine a plan of action.

My wife was at a women's retreat and the children were gone for the evening. What am I going to do all night? How do I wait out the hours knowing there is nothing I can do? I'm sure you've had that helpless feeling at one time or another.

The community we were living in at the time had one theater that featured one movie at a time. I decided to go. For 107 minutes my mind was occupied with the humorous comments, concoctions, and content. It wasn't a particularly good movie, but the humorous situations allowed me to soften, if only for a brief time, the emotional intensity I was feeling.

Over the next several days there were numerous sad, emotional, gut-wrenching times. I found myself attempting to interject humor at any point where it seemed the least bit appropriate. The chuckles and belly laughs eased the fear, reduced the stress, and brought comfort during some tense moments. As a family, we were able to divert our attention from the pain, fear, and curveball life had thrown. Humor wasn't a permanent fix, but it certainly provided temporary relief.

"I have seen what a laugh can do," Bob Hope reflected. "It can transform almost unbearable tears into something bearable, even hopeful."

Laughter is a cheap medicine. It distracts your attention, changes your attitude and outlook on life, causes relaxation and reduction of tension, while increasing the body's natural painkillers. In short, laughter relaxes our tensions and promotes a feeling of well-being. It allows us to take a brief sabbatical from the serious, the pain, and the tension. The ability to laugh is a sure sign of someone living a healthy life. It is a gift we give ourselves.

I like the way Josh Billings put it: "There ain't much fun in medicine, but there's a heck of a lot of medicine in fun." Norman Cousins also commented on another benefit of laughter. "I've never known a person," he said, "who possessed the gift of hearty laughter to be burdened by constipation." Sounds like a beneficial outcome to me.

Humor, and its sidekick laughter, have a few more benefits. They are tension reducers in times of change, emotional stabilizers during adversity, creativity stimulators, and marvelous reminders to live enthusiastically. Medically speaking, we know that laughter increases endorphins. Those little guys energize us and increase our endurance.

Mark my words, when a society has to resort to the lavatory for its humor, the writing is on the wall.

ALAN
BENNETT

UNSTRESS YOUR STRESS

Life is reduced to work, tasks, effort, an endless list of shoulds and musts . . . minus the necessary fun and laughter that keeps everything in perspective.

CHARLES SWINDOLL

HOW TO KEEP FROM BEING
WIRED AND TIRED

For far too many people, the stresses of life have zapped their ability to do their best, be their best, and enjoy their daily activities.

We can learn a marvelous lesson from the tightrope aerialist. Each move is made with precision and mastery, yet the casual observer may not recognize the key components for successful performance.

Aerialists focus primarily on maintaining balance. Each step is orchestrated by carefully touching their toes to the wire and keeping their eyes firmly planted on their goal.

Balance and focus are necessary to capitalize on the productive elements of stress and avoid being overwhelmed by negative stress.

Stress is an inside job! It's caused by what happens between your ears, by how you look at, think about, and respond to events.

JOHN NEWMAN, *How to Stay Calm & Collected When the Pressure's On*

STRESS-MANAGEMENT STRATEGIES

1. **Get in the driver's seat.** Emotionally healthy people tend to maintain a high degree of control over what happens in their life. Feeling in control helps reduce

feelings of stress. You may not be able to control life's events, people's demands, or work pressures, but you can decide how to respond to these situations.

2. **Passionately pursue your purpose.** An article in *Success* magazine noted, "Those who feel a sense of purpose and commitment, who view change as a challenge instead of a threat, aren't affected by stress in a negative way." A personal mission adds direction, meaning, and an empowering element during stressful times. Without purpose, stressful events throw us out of balance.

3. **Work your plan.** Take one thing at a time. Refrain from procrastinating. Complete uncompleted tasks. Choose how you spend your time. Determine your priorities and make sure they are built into your weekly schedule.

4. **Put problems in perspective.** Michael LeBoeuf believes, "Most stress is caused by people who overestimate the importance of their problems." Problems are unfortunate, but most are not catastrophic. Use your talents, abilities, strengths, and energy to make the best of those difficult situations. Break down problems into manageable pieces and go to work on resolution.

5. **Become a kookaburra.** A what? Kookaburras are Australian birds known for their deep laughing sound. When was the last time you had a good, belly-wrenching laugh? Preschoolers laugh an estimated 450 times a day; adults, 15 times a day. Who leads a more relaxed and healthy life? We lower our stress level every time we laugh.

6. **Don't strangle yourself.** "Worry" comes from the Anglo–Saxon, meaning to strangle or choke. Worry restricts your ability to think and act effectively. The best cure I know of for worry is action. When we do something about that which we are worried about, the unnecessary strangling effects of worry begin to lose their hold. Ralph Waldo Emerson put it this way: "Do the thing you fear the most, and the death of fear is certain."

7. **Listen to what you are saying.** Our self-talk and perceptions of events cause undue stress. We become what we think, and our perception of any event will determine our reaction to it. Never underestimate the power of the habitual thoughts, expectations, and beliefs you hold in your mind.

8. **Are we having fun yet?** Fun is a diversion from the norm that gets us out of the rut the stressors of life create. So, when was the last time you escaped the rut and had good, clean fun?

9. **Build a buddy system.** Focus on building quality relationships. Give up judging, criticizing, holding grudges, unnecessary competition, and the like. Earn your neighbor's love, say something nice to everyone you meet, help someone with one of their problems.

10. **Change your oil.** Most people take better care of their cars than they do themselves. To keep your body well tuned, learn to relax, take a recess, exercise, build an energy reserve through smart nutrition, recognize your limits, eliminate perfectionism and unrealistic expectations, and release emotions by talking with good friends.

11. **See streams in the desert.** Keep life in perspective. Concentrate on the positive. Approach failures and mistakes as opportunities. Develop and nurture your enthusiasm. See something good in every experience you have. Persevere in difficult times because better days are ahead. Every day is a new day. Life will always have its ups and downs.

A PRIMER ON MASTERING STRESS

S tress is a used, misused, abused, and overused word in our daily conversations. What really is stress? Dr. Hans Seyle, the father of stress-management research, said, "Stress is the wear and tear on your body caused by life's events." It is the body's physical, mental, and chemical reactions to circumstances that frighten, excite, confuse, endanger, and irritate.

Hundreds of experiences in life cause stress. These stressors create eustress (good stress) or distress (negative stress). Our bodies are designed to meet these stressors. However, each person must determine what is just the right amount of stress for him or her to function at his or her optimum level.

Experiencing too little stress causes irritability, boredom, dullness, and apathy. Too much stress can produce comparable results, along with feelings of being overwhelmed.

The most frequent causes of stress are an inability to adapt and not having an established code of behavior to guide our actions.

DR. HANS SEYLE

Dr. Seyle believed the most frequent causes of stress are an inability to adapt and not having an established code of behavior to guide our actions.

Adapt? Hundreds of thousands of years ago, this planet was populated by dinosaurs the size of which we have not seen since on this Earth. Then something happened. Within a relatively short period of time, virtually all of the beasts vanished.

Dinosaurs, with their inability to adapt to a changing world, became extinct.

Another creature lived during the dinosaur age. That species remains in existence today because of its ability to adapt. Frogs. Yes, those amphibious, adaptable creatures survived the changes.

Before we get too gung-ho about adapting, don't forget the second cause of stress: not having an established code of behavior to guide our actions.

In a laboratory experiment, frogs were placed in a shallow pan of room-temperature water. They were free to jump out of the pan at will. Under each pan was a Bunsen burner, which heated the water very gradually. As the temperature rose, the frogs adapted. Unfortunately, regardless of how hot the water became, the frogs never became uncomfortable enough to jump out of the pan.

So what happened? The frogs died because they did not have a code of behavior that told them to jump.

Likewise, we need to learn when enough is enough. Adapting is fine, but not without a code of behavior that warns us when it is time to jump. That same code is a warning signal that lets us know it is time to take action to deal with the stressors that now threaten our healthy existence.

Dr. Paul Rosch at the American Institute of Stress says, "The answer to stress management is to realize that stress is an unavoidable consequence of life." Stress is a given in life, but the impact on us is determined by how we respond to the experiences that cause stress.

Dealing with stress is an inside job. Adapt to it, learn from it, enjoy the positive results it can produce, but beware of getting burned by it.

I am so tired and I am crabby. There are enough nights when my husband and I are reduced to eating cheese rinds and tuna fish out of the can because we don't have anything in the refrigerator. I can't get the energy to cook, and I think, I'm going to lose this man over a tuna sandwich.

CANDICE
BERGEN

SURVIVAL OF THE STRESSED

*Some days you
tame the tiger.
And some days
the tiger has
you for lunch.*

TUG
MCGRAW

According to CNN, 28 percent of the American workforce voluntarily took pay cuts in 1998 to have more free time, less stress, and more balance in their lives.

The Associated Press recently reported the ulcer drug Prilosec® became the pharmaceutical industry's first $5-billion prescription medication. Prilosec® beat out the number-two cholesterol drug Zolor® by $1.1 billion and the highly publicized Viagra® by over $4 billion.

A study by the National Mental Health Association revealed the costs of depression in the workplace now exceed $40 billion annually.

Business Week estimates the cost to business of stress-related problems and mental illness is $150 billion annually in health insurance, disability claims, lost productivity, and other expenses.

These stress-related facts are enough to give you a headache—which is also quite common. An estimated 15 *tons* of aspirin are consumed every day.

The pace and condition of our lives is illustrated by the young mother who called a taxicab company late one afternoon. When the driver arrived, she brought out three young children and put them in the back seat. "Start the meter and I'll be back in a few minutes," she directed.

Twenty minutes later the woman returned and asked, "What do I owe you?"

The puzzled driver responded, "Aren't you going anyplace?"

"No," the woman replied. "I just needed a few quiet moments to myself."

Stressed? Irritable? Fatigued? Procrastinating? Stretched? Bored? Declining sense of humor? Emotionally tapped? Worried? Join the crowd. These consequences are reflected in lives struggling to maintain balance in an imbalanced world. "Reality," said Lily Tomlin, "is the leading cause of stress for those still in touch with it."

You've heard all the clichés. Stress is inevitable. If you are alive, you will experience stress. Life events or situations causing stress may be pleasant or unpleasant. You can't hide from it, run away from it, or eliminate it. Stress is the wear and tear of life. Your ability to deal effectively with stress is central to your personal and professional success. And all the world's people said, "Amen, now what?"

The last thing we need is to rehash what is already common knowledge about stress management. Volumes of stress-management material have been written over the last several years and, yet, the consequences continue to threaten our lives. We need to do something with all the information and knowledge we possess. Maybe we can provide a bit of practical assistance in fine tuning your stress management to move beyond survival into significant living.

The Concorde is a phenomenal aircraft. Tremendous heat is generated on the exterior of the plane as it flies at supersonic speed. The temperature on the external surface of the plane can reach 127 degrees Centigrade (261 degrees F) even though the outside air temperature is −56 degrees Centigrade (−69 degrees F).

This increased heat causes the plane to expand to 9 inches longer at cruising speed. The cabin floor of the airplane is uniquely designed on rollers and doesn't expand. A special air-conditioning system keeps the inside temperature constant.

While the outside of the Concorde experiences tremendous stress, the inside remains comfortable. The outer person is continually pressed, pushed, and pressured from every direction. You're required to expand to survive. And the ultimate challenge is to maintain inner courage, calm, and comfort.

The possibility of living healthier lives is within our grasp. It's not the condition of the world that gets us in trouble, but what we tell ourselves about the world. External events, circumstances, and demands can seem overwhelming, but what really matters is our condition inside.

Human behavior specialists have suggested for years that three fundamental actions are necessary to make changes in your life. First, you must believe that a change is needed. Second, you need to believe that you are the person who can change your life. Third, you need to believe that change is possible. Without these three beliefs, you will find it difficult to practice a lifestyle that gives you a sense of control.

I'm using the word LIFESTYLE as an acrostic for nine life-enhancing, career-enriching, stress-reducing principles. Check your personal thermometer against these benchmarks.

<u>L</u>isten to what your insides are telling you. Your head, heart, and stomach are built-in stress barometers. Recognizing the presence of stress and being sensitive to your body's warn-

ing signals will give you a head start on reducing the damage caused by stress. Avoiding the symptoms or pretending they don't exist is unwise, not to mention unhealthy.

People are often reluctant to admit they are experiencing increased fatigue, excessive anxiety, uncharacteristic moodiness, digestive problems, helplessness, or feelings of depression. The list could go on and on. When your body sends signals that something isn't right, listen. This is your alarm system. It doesn't always mean you're stressed, but it's a pretty good clue.

Insist on a proper perspective. Life's stressors can be overwhelming and to minimize the intensity of your challenges would be insensitive. However, each of us must recognize the tendency to blow a situation out of proportion by conjuring up in our mind the worst-possible scenario.

Earle Wilson defined perspective as, "The ability to see the present moment and immediate event against the background of a larger reference." Keep your imagination in check by focusing on the potential good results and viewing the current circumstances in light of the bigger picture. When life seems to be at its worst, take the time to discover the multitude of blessings you enjoy.

Forego what you can't control. People who frequently complain about feeling burned out are often those who expend considerable energy dealing with things over which they have no control. Their lives are driven by things, people, and events they can't do anything about. Dr. Paul Rosch advised, "Find what things you can have some control over, and come up with creative ways to take control."

Here's the irony. The best way to get in control is to give up control. Sometimes you have no control over a situation and it is a waste of psychological and physical energy to try to change what you cannot change. Accept it.

People who feel in control realize they always have control over how they will interpret or respond to the events. So, instead of giving control to their boss, crazy driver, the weather, financial challenges, unrealistic expectations, or demanding people, the in-control person determines a response they can control, that minimizes a painful result. Dr. Gerald Loren Fishkin said, "You can choose to see yourself as a helpless victim, pointing the finger of blame toward others, but being preoccupied with your role as a 'victim' blinds you to the opportunities that exist in every moment of your life."

End perfectionism. Perfectionism is a great way to increase stress. Where did you ever get the idea that you could be or should be perfect? Who told you everything in life had to go the way you had planned? There is a tremendous push to perform with excellence today, but that is a far cry from being perfect. Do your best with what you have. Be realistic about your own performance and the expectations you have of other people. Relax your standards. Have a forgiving spirit for undesirable events and people who disappoint you.

No matter what you think, you are not a Superperson able to leap tall buildings with a single bound and have the judges score you a perfect 10. "Admirable as the idea is," says Dr. George Stevenson in his *How to Deal with Your Tension,* "it is an open invitation to failure. No one can be perfect in everything. Decide which things you do well, and put your major effort into these . . . don't take yourself to task if you can't achieve the impossible."

Spiritual well-being precedes being well. This is a marvelous starting point. Some people tend to think their shoulders are broad enough to carry whatever load they encounter. Actually, once you turn everything over to God and allow

Him to work through you, incredible strength will surface to help you carry your portion of the load. The Bible says, "Cast all your anxieties on Him because He cares for you." It should be a relief to know that you're not expected to deal with pressures, stressors, and disappointments on your own.

Corrie ten Boom suffered miserably in concentration camps because she helped Jews escape from the Nazis. Her incredible faith allowed her to reflect: "I know that the experiences of our lives, when we let God use them, become the mysterious and perfect preparation for the work He will give us to do." That's spiritual well-being.

Talk to someone. Not just anyone. It should go without being said that you avoid negative, worrying, down-in-the-mouth people who will snuff out what little energy you have left. Preferably you will choose someone who is accepting, nonjudgmental, noncritical, and sincerely interested in your best interests. Find a respected listener with whom you can talk out your tensions.

Give up the pretense that seeking support is an admission of weakness. Quite the opposite is true. Only the strong have the courage to admit they don't have all the answers and are secure enough to seek out the wisdom of other people.

You are responsible. Jump-start your life by realizing no one is coming to your rescue. You are responsible for you. Rarely will your problems disappear by pretending they don't exist. If certain lifestyle patterns and behaviors are causing you difficulty, take responsibility for making the necessary adjustments. Don't wait for someone to come along to bail you out. You may wait for a long time with no satisfactory relief.

A prevailing mystery is why people continually indulge in behavioral, mental, and emotional activities that create unwanted stress in their lives. Either people believe what they are doing is actually healthy or they find it easier to wallow in their misery than to do something about it. If you want release from this vicious cycle, ask yourself, "What action can I take right now to make this situation better?" Then do it.

Look outward. An unfortunate consequence occurs when you become distressed. Your attention turns increasingly inward. Pondering your predicament and concentrating on yourself becomes an obsession. The minute you sense this is happening, reach out to help someone else. Dr. Hans Seyle, the respected stress specialist, put it this way, "Earn your neighbor's love."

Do one thing for someone everyday for which they cannot repay you. Focus on understanding rather than being understood, on loving rather than being loved. Count to 1,000 before saying or doing anything that could be hurtful to someone else. Go make things right with someone where tension has kept you from enjoying each other's company. Quit keeping score. Say, "I'm sorry, I was wrong." Celebrate others' successes. You'll be absolutely amazed how helping someone else will help to heal yourself.

Enjoy life. This is the ultimate catch-all principle. Enjoying life involves everything from doing absolutely nothing and learning to relax, to taking that vacation you've been putting off. Allow yourself to think positive thoughts, cultivate your sense of humor, and force yourself to have at least one good belly laugh everyday. Spend 90 percent of your time generating solutions for the problems you face and allow yourself to consider creative solutions that, until now, you were scared to try.

Take a hot bath or a cool shower, walk in the rain, run on the beach, breathe deep, enjoy a sunrise, savor a sunset, start a new hobby, revive an old one, treat yourself by buying that special item you've always wanted, sleep in, schedule "private time," and, probably most important, learn to live one day at a time.

People burn out, I suspect, not because they have too much to do, but because they get exhausted by the trivial and the inconsequential.

REV. LOUIS LOTZ

EMBRACING CHANGE

*Just because we cannot see clearly the
end of the road, that is no reason for not
setting out on the essential journey.
On the contrary, great change dominates
the world, and unless we move with change
we will become its victims.*

JOHN F. KENNEDY

ENJOY LIFE IN TIMES OF CHANGE

C hange is irritating. I dislike it. I resist it and, most of all, I want it to go away. As I write, our community leaders have decided to fix a road between my home and my office. There are other streets I can take, but I'm comfortable with my customary route. I continue to take the streets that run into the detour and am consistently upset when I reach the impassable road.

How most of us dread change, fight against it, or refuse to acknowledge it, even unto the last look in the coffin.

GWENDOLYN BROOKS

I know. I know. This minute irritation is nothing compared to the personal and professional changes you are experiencing. Yet, isn't it often the little things that get us? Expectations are unmet. Status quo is shattered. The comfort zone is suddenly pulled out from under us. Nothing seems simple anymore and we begin blowing things out of proportion.

It doesn't take a psychiatrist to tell us that we all desire a sense of normalcy in our lives. How often have you heard a co-worker, spouse, or friend say, "I can't wait for things to get back to normal." The truth is, things aren't going to get back to normal! Change is now the norm. It is a given. A way of life. To those who believe "This too shall pass!"—*sorry!* The world isn't going to suddenly stop changing so we can avoid ambiguity and uncertainty. We might as well learn to live with and enjoy life in these changing times.

Think about this. It is estimated the fund of information available to your profession doubles every five years. That means if you achieved a college degree more than five years ago, *you used to know a lot.*

Consider further that a weekday edition of the *New York Times* contains more information than the average person was likely to come across in a lifetime during the seventeenth century in England.

An estimated 100 scientific research papers will be published today.

My children presented me with a musical birthday card on my 40th birthday. I love gadgets, so I was intrigued every time I opened the card to hear it play "Happy Birthday." For two solid weeks I would test the endurance of this simple toy. I discarded it in the garbage can under the kitchen sink one night before going to bed. The next morning, I heard a faint musical sound as I entered the kitchen. Opening the door below the sink, I couldn't believe my ears. The card's power was dying but I could faintly hear it play the programmed tune. Some time later I learned that a $3.50 card contained more computer power than existed in the entire world before 1950.

Today, the watch you are wearing on your wrist contains more computer power than existed in the entire world prior to 1961. In fact, today's cars are powered by more computer technology than Apollo 11.

Times have certainly changed. Our lives can be compared to a daily scenario occurring in Africa. Every morning a gazelle wakes up and knows it must run faster today than the fastest lion, or be killed. At the same time, the hungry lion realizes it must run faster than the slowest gazelle, or go without a delicious meal. The moral: Whether a lion or gazelle, when the sun comes up, you'd better be running.

Sound familiar? We run faster and faster every day just to keep up with the harried pace required by life's changing nature. Yet, it seems we can't grow fast enough, or learn enough, or adapt quick enough to meet increasing demands on our time, energy, and mental stamina.

I've learned a couple of things during the road construction and other rapid life-altering changes. First, today is not guaranteed to be a repeat of yesterday. New signs, barricades, and detours pop up without warning. The world is moving too quickly for today to be a repeat of yesterday.

Second, the future is not what it used to be. Even the condition of the future changes as quickly as the ticks on the clock. Look back on the past year. You will undoubtedly notice many events transpired without advance notice or your approval. It seems almost impossible to predict what the future holds in store for us.

The Bureau of the Census concluded after a recent survey that "Change of all types—economic, social, cultural, technological, and political—is occurring at an increasing rate. In some areas, it is not merely accelerating but exploding. The rapid rate of change shows no sign of slowing in our lifetime."

That is a bit unsettling for us habitual types. No doubt about it, we are living in a time of accelerated, unavoidable, unrelenting, unsettling, uncontrollable, nonstop, unnerving change.

However, "Change is growth, both intellectual and emotional," says Dr. Joyce Brothers. "People who are open to change enjoy life far more than those who are bogged down in static status quo."

I've finally concluded that the future belongs to those who not only accept change, but embrace it, enjoy it, and use it to create their future. It is time to abandon or modify what isn't working anymore. Of course, even the stuff that is good enough today probably won't be tomorrow.

Change dispenses with stability, status quo, and the much-beloved comfort zone. People and organizations must learn how to use change and actively participate in it. It is no longer realistic to just cope with change. The choice is to have change forced upon us or use it to stake our claim in the future. That takes courage!

The challenges of the twenty-first century to deal with the crucial changes needed to move us forward, while maintaining balance in life, are immense. It can be done, but not without embracing a new revolution.

There are three possible responses to this challenge. There will be those who are on the forefront of the revolution. Others will follow it, and still another group will sleep through it while hoping things will soon get back to normal. The sleepers are in trouble and the followers run the risk of being left in the dust or getting stuck in what the revolutionaries leave behind. Both the sleepers and the followers just keep falling further behind. As someone once said, "You can't leave foot-prints in the sands of time if you're sitting on your butt. And, who wants to leave butt prints in the sands of time?"

Don't be too hard on the sleepers and followers, but these sleepers and followers need a wake-up call. Most of what we are taught throughout our early lives is about how to keep things comfortable, secure, and void of undo surprises. It's difficult to forget or to put our lifelong conditioning out of our minds and break the old rules to create new ideas.

Leading a personal revolution requires a recommit-ment of the mind and heart, along with an enlarged vision of what the future can be. You'll need to fill your tool box with renewed insight and understanding of life's demands. Rethink the present, create new ways of doing things, reinvent pres-ent processes, and let go of the past.

It is ludicrous to think anyone can survive, let alone thrive professionally, without a personal transformation that breeds an optimistic, adventurous outlook toward the future. The moment you commit to such a lifestyle, doors of oppor-tunity begin to open. Otherwise, cynicism, pessimism, and fatalism rear their ugly heads. Stress elevates. Desperation levels rise. You disempower yourself. Self-pity reigns.

Facing the rugged terrain of your upcoming journey requires paying a price. Experiencing success in these turbulent times is unlikely without a personal devotion to modify the way we do things. Rather than wasting incredible energy fighting change, holding on to old habits, and resisting new processes, invest your energies in finding ways to align yourself with the changes.

Please realize that if you don't create your future, someone else will. The best way to influence your tomorrow is to make the most of today.

GIVE OF YOURSELF

*There is no
more noble
occupation
in the world
than to assist
another human
being—to
help someone
succeed.*

ALAN LOY
MCGINNIS

❋

Humankind's reflex reaction to change is to focus on *me.* "What's in it for me?" "How will my life be affected?" "Why do all the changes occur in my department?" Such questions become prevalent.

Self-pity parties are scheduled. Human spirits begin to wilt. You begin feeling like the whole world is against you. The devastating affects of change are given permission to take their toll. *Stop.* When was the last time you took an inventory of what you've unselfishly given to others instead of what you thought you should receive from them? How have you given of yourself to someone else this week without expecting anything in return?

I've learned much about this subject from Jimmy Carter. He dreamed of being Governor of Georgia and then aspired to the U.S. Presidency. His dreams were fulfilled until world events changed. The Iran hostage crisis erupted and ultimately resulted in a sour end to Carter's presidency. Then what?

Jimmy and Rosalynn dedicated themselves to a new dream of helping the poor through Habitat for Humanity. By building low-cost housing for the poor, the Carters rebounded from disappointment to find excitement and fulfillment in helping others.

Dreams do get demolished. Life can seem unfair. Adversity and calamity surround us. Yet in the midst of it all, the Natural Laws of this universe remain intact.

One of those laws, the law of reciprocity, indicates that when I help others deal with change, be successful, feel better about life, or work through adversity, my life will be enriched as well. You've heard it before. What you give, you get. What you send out comes back. What you sow, you reap.

Rent the movie *An Officer and a Gentleman.* In it, the hero performs poorly in naval officer training. He is in constant conflict with his superiors. Contrary to military regulations, he shines the shoes of his classmates for money. But, he shines when it comes to performing the obstacle course. It's as if the course was designed for his abilities and it appears that he has a shot at setting a training record when the class is required to run it for an official time.

The story line really becomes interesting when the soldier's best friend commits suicide and he challenges the noncommissioned officer in charge of his training. He is certain to be kicked out of officer training. However, while his dismissal is pending, his class runs the obstacle course.

One of his classmates is a woman who struggles climbing over one of the obstacles. As the hero pursues an obstacle course record, his classmate becomes stuck on the difficult obstacle. It's the hero's decision-making moment. What should he do? The only thing he had impressed his superiors with was his obstacle-course performance. Perhaps if he could set the record, he would not be dismissed from officer training.

Then the unbelievable occurs. The hero stops and rushes back to help his classmate, though he knows this will cost him the record he was destined to set.

This one act of helping someone else results in the powers that be allowing him to graduate and become an "officer and a gentleman."

Convincing people in times of change that the best way to increase the quality of their life is do something that will enhance another person's life is difficult. Attention tends to turn inward and get stuck there. Selfishness takes its ugly seat and we become occupied with filling our own needs. Just the opposite action is needed to get in tune with what's good for us.

Like an officer and a gentleman, we need to reach out unselfishly to help others overcome the obstacles that keep them from being successful. Then we can experience the benefit of the Peace Corps advertisement: "Feel better about yourself than you ever thought possible."

We cannot hold a torch to light another's path without brightening our own.

BEN
SWEETLAND

COMMIT YOURSELF TO A
CHANGE-READY LIFESTYLE

The status quo
sets on society
like fat on cold
chicken soup
and it is quite
content to be
what it is.
Unless someone
comes along to
stir things up
there just
won't be
change.

ABIE
HOFFMAN

In the opening chapter of *Tom Sawyer,* Mark Twain shares an interesting conversation that reflects the condition of human nature. Tom tries to persuade his friend Huck to join him in his plans to form a band of robbers and to take captives, much like pirates used to do.

Huck asks Tom what pirates do with the captives they take, and Tom answers, "Ransom them." "Ransom? What's that?" asks Huck. "I don't know. But that's what they do. I seen it in books; and so of course that's what we got to do," explains Tom. "Do you want to go doing different from what's in the books, and get things all muddled up?"

This dialogue represents a way of thinking that's not much different from many people today. It is easier to do what we have always been doing even though the times require we evaluate, refine, and speed up the things we do. The beliefs of the past shackle us from moving into the future. Unfortunately, like Tom Sawyer, we may not know what we are doing or why, but that's the way it has always been done. So, we blindly follow the traditions of the past.

Instead of attempting to live in a future that is a repeat of yesterday's strategies, abundant opportunities await those who are creative and resilient in these chaotic times. We are designed to encounter life most effectively when we grow at a pace that allows us to stay abreast of the major changes we face. When your life is challenging, but productive and fulfilling, there's evidence you are keeping up with and assimilating the changes you face.

Dean Rusk, former U.S. Secretary of State, said, "The pace of events is moving so fast that unless we can find some way to keep our sights on tomorrow, we cannot expect to be in touch with today." The best way to be prepared for an ever-changing tomorrow is to implement a daily growing plan today.

Being change-sensitive and change-ready is not achieved by the snap of your fingers. Overnight express delivery isn't an option. The major challenge is to continually evaluate our thinking. Futurist Faith Popcorn predicted in *The Popcorn Report,* "If you thought it yesterday, if you're thinking it today, you won't think it tomorrow."

To sharpen our thinking and be continually in tune with change demands, we need to nurture an ongoing attitude that is:

- open to new ideas
- willing to explore new techniques and discard worn-out beliefs
- excited about learning
- committed to facing challenges and discovering opportunities
- flexible
- prepared to leave the past and enter the future
- constantly prepared to adjust perceptions, practices, and performance

Change-agent master Rosabeth Moss Kanter believes, "The individuals who will succeed and flourish will also be masters of change: adept at reorienting their own and others' activities in untried directions to bring about higher levels of achievement. They will be able to acquire and use power to produce innovation."

What habits, limiting beliefs, procedures, attitudes, self-limiting thoughts are getting in the way? For goodness sake, let them go. As Eddy Ketchursid aptly stated, "If your horse is dead, for goodness sake—dismount!" If you have been doing something a particular way for 5 or 10 years, it's a pretty good sign, in these changing times, that you haven't prepared to master the future. Not to replace them is professional and personal suicide.

Create a clean sheet today and decide exactly what you will be doing tomorrow, and in the weeks and months to come, to keep you on the cutting edge of life's accelerating and complex change.

He who rejects change is the architect of decay. The only human institution which rejects progress is the cemetery.

HAROLD
WILSON

SEEK
NEW HORIZONS

Too often the opportunity knocks, but
by the time you disengage the chain, push
back the bolt, unhook the two locks and
shut off the burglar alarms, it's too late.

RITA COOLIDGE

NOTICE THE OPPORTUNITIES

Jack Welch, CEO of General Electric, encourages us to "Stimulate and relish change. Don't be frightened or paralyzed by it. See change as an opportunity, not just a threat."

If you see change as a threat, there is a tendency to become defensive, irrational, and prone to discouragement. Finger-pointing, blaming, and complaining become the order of the day. People go home drained and discouraged because their energies are spent on fighting the perceived negative impact of change. As a result, hundreds of opportunities are lost because their focus is blurred, causing them to be blind to positive possibilities.

If, on the other hand, change is viewed as an opportunity, you set in motion constructive behavior that can make change your ally. Every situation you encounter can become an opportunity. Excitement is the prerequisite to uncovering possibilities and generating options. Energy is multiplied when passion becomes a part of the formula.

You create your own opportunities out of the same raw materials from which other people create their defeats.

BERNIE SIEGEL, M.D.

When change is happening all around you, stop and reexamine where you are going and what you are encountering. Learn to draw out of life's events valuable nuggets leading you to golden opportunities. Greek philosopher Plutarch wrote, "As bees extract honey from thyme, the strongest and driest of herbs, so sensible men often get advantage and profit from the most awkward circumstances."

Roy Speer and Lowell Paxson capitalized on their observations of people's lifestyles. They found: 1. People like to shop. 2. People like to watch TV. 3. People like to shop or watch TV anytime they please. These simple conclusions led to the development of The Home Shopping Network, Inc., a 24-hour-a-day TV shopping channel. Speaking of extracting honey, this little venture appealed to TV watchers and shoppers everywhere, generating hundreds of millions of dollars in revenue annually.

This opportunistic approach led Walt Disney to reinvent the amusement park. With it, Ted Turner revolutionized cable television. Colonel Sanders helped launch a multibillion-dollar fast-food industry. Bill Gates catapulted into computer software stardom. Sam Walton created his "always the low price" Wal-Mart shopping experience.

Being prepared to capitalize on opportunities is an ongoing venture. There is no such thing as attaining and resting. We are constantly determining what we need next to remain effective. Invest in some reflection time. Reappraise your learning curve. What resources have you accessed? Are there untapped energy reserves?

First ask yourself, "What presently works for me that I need to continue doing to create the ideal future?" Then, "What elements of my present and past need to be discarded?" What excess baggage hinders you from achieving and experiencing what you want in life? Snakes shed their skin as they outgrow it. People need to shed themselves of habits that have outlived their usefulness or inhibit the pursuit of new possibilities. "Equilibrium is death," said Kevin Kelly. "Seek persistent equilibrium." Therein exists the entrance to a refreshing and expanded view of change.

Expect to strain a little. Straining and stretching increase our flexibility. Doing only what comes easily or naturally gets us nowhere, and more than likely produces little more than treading water or even losing ground.

Heed the words of Alexander Graham Bell: "When one door closes, another one opens. But we look so long and regretfully upon the closed door that we do not see the one that has opened for us."

MOVE BOLDLY INTO THE UNKNOWN

To risk is to loosen your grip on the known and the certain, and to reach for something you are not entirely sure of but you believe is better than what you now have, or is at least necessary to survive. Taking a risk is central to everything worthwhile in life.

DAVID
VISCOTT

Fifty years ago Akio Morita and another man started a new company called Tokyo Telecommunications Engineering in a bombed-out department store in Tokyo.

Ten years later, the company introduced the world to the first transistor radio. An American company, Bulova, knew opportunity when they saw it and offered to buy the radios at a tempting profit. Mr. Morita hesitated to accept the offer because the radios would be sold under the Bulova name.

According to a 1994 *USA Today* article entitled "Sony's Legend Stepping Down," Morita wanted to establish his own company's brand name. So even though the deal would have brought his struggling company an infusion of much needed cash, Morita decided against the deal, informing the executives at Bulova, "I am now taking the first step for the next 50 years of my company."

Morita's bold move helped his company to become one of the greatest success stories in business. They introduced the world to such innovative products as the VCR and compact disc players. Today, they have diversified into a number of products and business ventures and their name is synonymous with innovation and quality. Remember Mr. Morita's decision to forego the sure thing by risking his future every time you see the brand name "Sony."

"It is our destiny to move out," said Louis L'Amour, "to accept the challenge, to dare the unknown. . . ." This advice tends to unsettle human nature. Akio Morita's experience is an example of one who defied the pull of an inviting offer to reach for something that wasn't a sure thing. How about you? Rather than accepting security by knowing what tomorrow will bring, or the boredom of knowing what the day after tomorrow will bring, how about moving boldly in the direction of adventurous living.

The story is told of a spy who was captured and sentenced to death by a general in the Persian army. Before execution, the general would engage in a rather unusual procedure. He would offer the captor a choice between the firing squad or a big, black door.

The spy was surprised at the offer and deliberated on his choice for a long time until finally deciding on the firing squad. Moments later, his life was over.

The general turned to his aide and said, "They always prefer the known to the unknown. Yet, we give them a choice."

The aide himself was unaware of what consequences exist beyond the big, black door so he asked his commander. "Freedom," replied the general, "and I've only known a few brave enough to take it."

How comfortable and almost automatic it is to become preoccupied with the familiar and satisfied with what is. Leaving the security blanket behind and venturing into the unknown is scary, yet continually playing it safe is boring. We need a balance, an expanded menu of options that tempt our taste buds.

It's a test to let go and enjoy whatever potentialities this day will bring. I understand how risky it is for people to leap outside the box of status quo. Fortunately, I'm learning how exciting it can be to expose yourself to the unknown—not recklessly but with calculated enthusiasm, so that you can enjoy the possibilities. Some of the things I enjoy the most now are things that I was initially fearful of trying, simply because I didn't want to appear clumsy, inept, or uneducated. This isn't really taking a chance; it's giving yourself a chance to test your limits, to prove what you can do.

To get you started, follow the advice of Virgil Thomson who said, "Try a thing you haven't done three times. Once, to get over the fear of doing it. Twice, to learn how to do it. And a third time to figure out whether you like it or not."

Are you primed to try out some wild ideas? How about breaking out of your old routines and doing something different. Extend yourself. Put some adventure in your approach to handling things instead of relying on conventional means. Give yourself permission to explore, to move forward without the guarantee of success. You can't really avoid risk so why not stretch yourself and see what opportunities you've been ignoring. The worst that can happen is that you won't get what you're accustomed to getting.

Will the fear go away? Probably not. Dr. Susan Jeffries observed, "As long as I continue to push out into the world, as long as I continue to stretch my capabilities, as long as I continue to take risks in making my dreams come true, I am going to experience fear." There will be a recurring fear of failing or embarrassment. The fears of rejection, uncertainty, and disappointment will rear their ugly heads. Even the fear of difficulty will threaten. The desire for safety will continually tempt you to stop where you are and rely on old faithful. Don't let it get to you.

Thoughts to enhance your risk-taking:

1. **Other people have been where you're thinking of going.** Let that knowledge inspire your spirit to take the journey.

2. **It can't be that bad.** Ask yourself: "What have I got to lose?" Accept the fact that you won't necessarily like or succeed at everything you try, but you'll undoubtedly learn a lot. If you can handle the worst possible outcome, take the risk.

3. **You can do it!** Bruce Barton said, "Nothing splendid has ever been achieved except by those who dared believe that something inside them was superior to circumstances." There is a direct correlation between your self-image and risk quotient. Break through your self-constructed ceiling of limitations and realize you can progress past where you are. Challenge your self-doubts and you'll grow stronger.

4. **No matter what, you will benefit.** Risk-takers who win or lose learn to focus on the process as well as results. They learn to rise above what doesn't work and find another way to be successful. They see possibilities and opportunities that propel them past the status quo and mediocrity. They experience the challenge of sacrifice and the satisfaction of solutions.

Living at risk is jumping off the cliff and building your wings on the way down.

R A Y
B R A D B U R Y

"The world is full of wonders, riches, powers, puzzles," said Toni Flures. "What it holds can make us horrified, sorrowful, amazed, confused, joyful. But nothing can make us bored. Boredom is the result of some pinch in ourselves, not of some lack in the world." Boredom is the unconscious friend of those who fail to experience the world's wonders. Don't become so caught up in your small world that you fail to take advantage of opportunities available to you. Allow security to remain a stranger and risk to become your friend.

THE FUN IS IN THE
CHALLENGE

*You can
always tell
when you are
on the road
to success;
it's uphill
all the way.*

PAUL
HARVEY

❋

Tom Monaghan was born in Ann Arbor, Michigan in 1937. His father died when Tom was 4 years old and he grew up in foster homes, orphanages, and finally a detention home for delinquent children. He attempted to pursue his childhood dream of becoming a priest but was kicked out of a seminary, forcing him to look at other career options. After a short stint at Ferris State College, Monaghan ran out of money and enlisted in the Marine Corps.

During his transition back to civilian life, Monaghan's brother suggested they buy a pizza parlor call Dominick's in Ypsilanti; so Tom borrowed the money and became an instant entrepreneur. The years that followed were challenging to say the least. His brother wanted out of the partnership. A new partner embezzled enough money to leave Monaghan broke, and he was forced to change the name of the company to Domino's. His original store burned. Domino's went public, resulting in near financial collapse, and then the Domino's sugar people sued him for infringing on their name. A 5-year, $1.5-million fight won him the right to maintain Domino's as his company's name. Hundreds of stores were added to the Domino's chain and Monaghan amassed a fortune.

Tom Monaghan's character was revealed in a visit he persisted to set up with his idol Ray Kroc, founder of McDonald's. Kroc grilled him with questions about his operation and then leaned forward in his chair and said, "I'm going to give you some advice. You have made it now. You can do anything you want; make all the money you can possibly spend. So what I think you should do now is slow down. Take it easy. Open a few stores every year, but be very careful. Play it safe."

Monaghan was dumbfounded. How could his entrepreneurial hero suggest such a thing? Finally he blurted out, "But that wouldn't be any fun!"

A brief moment of silence seemed like an eternity and then Kroc smiled and responded, "That's just what I hoped you would say!"

Struggles, challenges, dreams, obstacles, and setbacks are all a part of the fun and satisfaction on the road to success. Only those intent on making the journey as enjoyable as the destination can endorse such a courageous pursuit.

If you wish success in life, make perseverance your bosom friend, experience your wise counselor, caution your elder brother and hope your guardian genius.

JOSEPH ADDISON

TOO FAT TO FLY

*Progress is
a tide. If we
stand still
we will surely
be drowned.
To stay on
the crest,
we have to
keep moving.*

HAROLD
MAYFIELD

Innovators, entrepreneurs, and adventure seekers all know the road ahead is filled with uncertainties. If they waited for the conditions to be perfect, they would never pursue their dreams. They are also keenly aware how quickly atrophy sets in if they are not constantly moving toward their goals.

The great Danish philosopher Søren Kierkegaard once told a story of a flock of geese that was starting to head South to escape the blast of wintry winds. The first night they landed in a farmer's yard and filled themselves with corn. Next morning they flew on—all, that is, except one. "The corn is good," this big goose said, "so I will stay and enjoy it another day." The next morning he decided to wait still another day, and another after that, enjoying the delicious food. Pretty soon he had developed a habit. "Tomorrow I will fly South," he said.

Then came the inevitable day when the winds of winter were so severe that waiting longer would mean death in the frozen wastes. So he stretched his wings and waddled across the barnyard, picking up speed as he went. But alas! He was too fat to fly. He had waited too long.

Enjoying the fruits of past labors. Coming upon unexpected satisfying experiences. Achieving a personal goal. Making a huge sale. Getting that long-awaited promotion. These types of experiences tend to create two opposing reactions. Some people develop a greater passion for action and a desire to outdo what they did before. Still others become so comfortable that a severe case of stagnation sets in. Any person who spends too long enjoying what they did without maintaining a steady diet of action will soon find themselves stale, disinterested, and unprepared to face the next challenge.

Remember this: Untalented, mediocre people who fully apply themselves go further than the superior people who don't. Since each positive, progressive action you take propels you closer to desirable rewards and outcomes, the sooner you begin, the better.

Thomas Edison was right. "Everything comes to he who hustles while he waits." It's not what you're going to do when things start going your way, but it's what you're doing now.

Success is not the result of spontaneous combustion. You must set yourself on fire.

REGGIE LEACH

CULTIVATE A
FUN SPIRIT

*We don't stop laughing because we grow old,
we grow old because we quit laughing.*

LEO BUSCAGLIA

RENEW THE CHILD
IN YOU

Alvin Schwartz said, "Laughter is the natural sound of childhood." Visit your local preschool and you'll quickly discover that statement is true. Remember those days? Reviving that childlike spirit will reap substantial adult benefits.

To be fun and have fun has proven instrumental in fostering creativity, enhancing problem-solving, and increasing retention in the classroom. An absence of fun can reduce productivity, increase job turnover, and have an acute negative influence on morale. Injecting a childlike spirit in all facets of life increases enjoyment.

Maintaining a sense of childlike behavior should be a lifelong pursuit. Children too soon are told to grow up, to act like an adult. So, what do they do? Life gets heavy. Playfulness deteriorates. Problems are catastrophized. They start seeking artificial and sometimes inappropriate ways to escape from the drudgery of adulthood. Do we really want children to

Realize that a sense of humor is deeper than laughter and more satisfying than comedy and delivers more rewards than merely being entertaining. A sense of humor sees the fun in everyday experiences. It is more important to have fun than it is to be funny.

LAURENCE J. PETER *and* BILL DANA

begin acting like adults, or would it be better for adults to recapture a bit of their childhood spirit?

I want my children to leave home some day (most of you are agreeing with that point) and tell their friends about how much fun it was living in our home. It wasn't fun because we were childish, but we approached our relationships, mealtimes, family trips, holidays, and life in general with a spirit of joy and playfulness. Work wasn't a drudgery for Mom and Dad; our children saw a passion for what we did. Their childhood dreams, school events, personal endeavors, difficult decisions, and complicated relationships and other activities were all viewed as opportunities to create fullness in their lives.

A childlike spirit produces creativity, fun, productivity, and a desire to get up and do it all over again tomorrow. That's why young children rarely need much prodding to get them going in the morning. Of course, once we introduce them to an alarm clock, they immediately recognize that getting up in the morning is certainly not meant to be a joyous occasion. Thus, we begin one of the dreaded journeys into adulthood.

As you observe and experience life, ask yourself: "How would a preschooler respond?" This simple exercise is certain to brighten what you see. "When you discard arrogance, complexity and a few other things that can get in the way," advises *Tao of the Pooh* author Benjamin Hoff, "sooner or later you will discover that simple, childlike and mysterious secret . . . Life is Fun."

Look for humor everywhere you go. Create reasons for laughter or laugh for no reason at all. Spread your sense of joy around. It will not only enrich your life but draw people closer to you and improve their lives as well.

I am well aware that the ability to laugh or see the world through humorous eyes is not for everybody. In fact, I recommend only those who want to have fun, enjoy their life, and feel alive, consider such an outrageous recommendation to *loosen up . . . lighten up . . . and live it up.*

LISTEN FOR LIFE'S LAUGHABLE
MOMENTS

*Everything
is funny as
long as it's
happening to
somebody else.*

WILL
ROGERS

❋

From the boardroom to the bedroom, the office to the bathroom orifice, main street to the airways, life's laughable moments are everywhere. Expect the unexpected. Open your eyes to the abnormal. Let your ears hear the humor. Allow your heart to overflow with laughter. Look for at least one situation each day for which you can enjoy a hearty burst of laughter.

Looking for these laughable moments is a skill Linda Ellerbee learned when dealing with the devastating news she had breast cancer. The discovery was made in 1992 and a double mastectomy ordered to save her life.

That summer Linda bought some breast prostheses to use while swimming. Instead of fastening them to her skin with Velcro as the directions instructed, she simply inserted the prostheses into her bathing suit. When she came out of the water, one had made its way around to her back. "Now," said Linda, "you can either laugh at such a thing or cry your eyes out." She decided to laugh.

Ms. Ellerbee was quoted as saying, "I have always felt that laughter in the face of reality is probably the finest sound there is and will last until the day when the game is called on account of darkness. In this world, a good time to laugh is any time you can."

Laughable moments occur daily. Whether you laugh or cry depends entirely on your ability to think funny and, oftentimes, laugh at yourself. Capitalizing on the laughable moments can help you play enthusiastically, live gracefully, endure the pressures of change, and remain resilient when adversity rears its ugly head.

Laughter isn't a cure-all. I've often compared it to changing a baby's dirty diaper: It isn't a permanent solution but it sure makes things better for a while.

Listen for the subtle, soft, and simple laughter moments.

A chuckle a day may not keep the doctor away, but it sure does make those times in Life's waiting room a little more bearable.

ANNE WILSON SCHAEF

THINK FUNNY

*Laughter is
the most
powerful
state of mind
there is.
When you're
laughing, you
can't think of
anything else.*

H. JACKSON
BROWN

L ife has a bountiful amount of difficult and serious moments. Our job is to find responses that keep life in perspective. Begin to view your stressful experiences as a source of laughter material. Change provides bountiful reasons to be upset, worried, and confused. Find ways to laugh at the craziness and absurdity of it all.

In 1981 President Ronald Reagan was shot by a would-be assassin. As his condition was being evaluated by medical personnel, he reportedly looked up and responded, "I hope you're all Republicans." His ability to think funny helped President Reagan relieve the tension of a nation concerned about his condition.

On another occasion President and Mrs. Reagan appeared on "Good Morning America." Mrs. Reagan was close to the edge of the stage and suddenly fell off. Startled by the unexpected event, a number of people rushed over to offer assistance while the President watched. Once he was assured she was okay, President Reagan looked over at her and said, "Nancy, I told you not to fall off the platform unless I wasn't getting any applause."

It is important to remember that what we think about will determine our reactions. "Thinking funny" does not mean every event is a "ha-ha" experience. Psychological research verifies that humor is good therapy. It helps you keep life in perspective. So, "thinking funny" is a choice to see the bright side.

I remember an especially trying time during my college years (I think the trying time lasted about four years) when my roommate finally chided me, "Cheer up, things could get worse." I did cheer up and sure enough, things got worse.

Thinking funny won't keep you from getting hit by trouble and difficulties. It won't insure that the road ahead will be void of hills and valleys, but it will give you the psychological boost you need to handle the ups and downs.

Thinking funny involves training your mind to see the light side of the dark side of life. Laugh or cry. It's a choice. Crying cleanses the tear ducts, but laughter encourages the soul.

James Russell Lowell possessed a lighthearted attitude about growing old. While passing a building on the outskirts

Sometimes you just need to look reality in the eye, and deny it.

GARRISON KEILLOR

❊

of Boston, he noticed a sign reading, "Home for Incurable Children." Turning to a friend, he remarked, "They'll get me in there some day."

How about the lady experiencing a particularly frustrating round of golf. Back in the clubhouse she laments: "I finally figured out my problem. I was standing too close to the ball . . . after I hit it."

Lighten up . . . Think funny!

BE WILLING TO LAUGH
AT YOURSELF

D
r. John Maxwell had this observation: "One of the most liberating experiences of life is to be able to laugh at yourself. When you lose that ability, everything in life takes on a much too serious complexion. I've discovered that a lot of my idiosyncrasies can either be a cause for despair or hilarity. I've decided to choose the latter. Life is strangely funny if you don't have your value or sense of adequacy tied up in being perfect."

If I were given the opportunity to present a gift to the next generation it would be the ability for each individual to learn to laugh at himself.

CHARLES
SCHULZ

"Humor is an attitude, a way of looking at the world," says humor expert Joel Goodman. "Laughter is a way of expressing humor." How do you see your world? How do you express it? Can the people closest to you recognize how much you love life by your ability to laugh at yourself?

G. K. Chesterton spoke to the sourpusses of this world when he wrote, "Madmen are always serious; they go mad from lack of humor." Maybe that's why I admire guys like the vertically challenged (short) wanna-be cowboy who quit wearing cowboy boots. He kidded others that the boots gave him a rash . . . under his armpits. This attitude reflects the most refined sense of humor—the ability to laugh at ourselves.

I've been bald for many years. I know every bald joke there is, yet there is always somebody who wants to share a bit of their jocular wisdom with me. "Grass doesn't grow on busy streets." "Bald in the front, you're a thinker. Bald in the back, you're a lover. Bald all over, you only think you're a lover." "God only covers that which he doesn't like." "I may have lost the waves, but I still have the beach." I'm sure you've heard them all as well.

You know what? I laugh every time someone decides to entertain me with these worn-out, overused, clichés. Why? Why not? I like to laugh. It sure beats crawling in a corner and lamenting my follicle challenge.

Think of all the failures, stumbling blocks, embarrassing moments, and down-right stupid things you've experienced. Now recall how six months later, you laughed about them (or should have). John Powell observed: "He who has learned to laugh at himself shall never cease to be entertained."

One final word of encouragement and admonition from Ethel Barrymore. "You grow up," she said, "the day you have the first real laugh—at yourself."

We're only young once, but with humor, we can be immature forever.

ART GLINER

MAKE THE BEST
OF THE WORST

*When you make a mistake, don't look back
at it long. Take the reason of the thing into
your mind, and then look forward. Mistakes
are lessons of wisdom. The past cannot be
changed. The future is yet in your power.*

HUGH WHITE

DON'T BEAT UP YOURSELF

A "Peanuts" cartoon features Charlie Brown reflecting, "Sometimes I lie awake at night, and ask, 'Where have I gone wrong?' Then a voice says to me, 'This is going to take more than one night.'"

I can relate to Charlie Brown's personal discovery. If mistakes could be credited toward formal degrees, my walls would be filled with diplomas. At the same time, I agree with Sophia Loren that "Mistakes are part of the dues one pays for a full life." Although painful at times, a lifetime of mistakes indicates you've lived life to the fullest and have accumulated a collection of valuable experiences.

If you are stretching to improve the quality of your life, mistakes are imminent. You simply cannot step into a world of unknowns and expect to make accurate, perfectly judged decisions. The margin of error is high for people refusing to endorse a life of complacency. If you only rely on past experiences and rehashing old ideas to push you forward, you're

To err is human . . . but when the eraser wears out ahead of the pencil, you're overdoing it.

JERRY JENKINS

*A doctor can
bury his
mistakes but
an architect
can only
advise his
client to
plant vines.*

FRANK LLOYD
WRIGHT

❋

going to miss the excitement of expanding your thinking and capturing the adventure of living. In fact, you'll probably find yourself wandering in circles, recycling the same regimen of activities and information. Experimentation lights new fires critical for peak performance.

Coach Paul "Bear" Bryant had a simplistic, yet effective strategy for dealing with mistakes. He said, "When you make a mistake, there are only three things you should ever do about it: (1) Admit it. (2) Learn from it. (3) Don't repeat it."

1. Admit your mistakes. Although Malcolm Forbes might have been right that "Correcting mistakes swiftly is more important than admitting them," the first step is actually admitting you made a mistake. "No man has a chance to enjoy permanent success," asserted Napoleon Hill, "until he begins to look in a mirror for the real cause of all his mistakes." Everyone makes mistakes and being honest with yourself and others saves energy and speeds up the process for repairing the damages. History teaches that an attempted coverup will ultimately label you deceptive.

Remember in July of 1994 when Intel discovered that its Pentium processing chip had a flaw? Although the chip occasionally computed wrong answers for division problems using large numbers, Intel determined the flaw would only affect the average user once every 27,000 years. Rather than fix or expose the flaw, Intel continued to promote and aggressively sell the defective computer chip.

Within five months, rumors of the flaw spread throughout the computer world. Intel's coverup was exposed, but they continued to downplay the significance. A dramatic step by IBM to stop selling units with the Pentium chip finally got Intel's attention and they agreed to exchange the chips when requested. Coming clean ultimately helped the company reclaim their positive image.

Winston Churchill endorsed the belief that "If you simply take up the attitude of defending a mistake, there will be no hope for improvement." Coverups aggravate the mistake. Admission is the beginning point of correction.

2. Learn from your mistakes. Your blunders and bloopers are a natural part of life and learning. Life is a trial-and-error process and the imperfectness of this process will inevitably produce mistakes. Face it, sometimes the best way to learn the right way of doing things is to first do it the wrong way. Of course, we can't continue doing things the wrong way and just conclude it isn't working.

Dale Carnegie believed, "The successful man will profit from his mistakes and try again in a different way."

The following humorous story was e-mailed to me a few months ago. The weather was very hot and a man wanted to take a dive in a nearby lake. He didn't bring his swimsuit, but who cared? He was all alone. So he undressed and got into the water.

After some delightful minutes of cool swimming, a pair of elderly ladies walked onto the shore in his direction. He panicked, got out of the water, and grabbed a bucket lying in the sand nearby. He held the bucket in front of himself and sighed with relief.

The ladies got nearby and looked at him. He felt awkward and wanted to move. Then one of the ladies said, "You know, I have a special gift. I can read minds."

"Impossible," said the embarrassed man, "you really know what I think?"

"Yes," the lady replied. "Right now, I bet you think that the bucket you're holding has a bottom."

Mistakes often expose our private feelings, weaknesses, or careless actions. The embarrassment can make it difficult to step back, look at the situation objectively, and determine we will do differently the next time around.

"When I reflect, as I frequently do, upon the felicity I have enjoyed," Benjamin Franklin pondered, "I sometimes say to myself, that were the offer made me, I would engage to run again, from beginning to end, the same career of life. All I would ask, should be the privilege of an author to correct in a second edition, certain errors of the first."

Your "second edition" can begin the moment you take responsibility for an error and determine what you have learned to enrich your life. Commit yourself to be big enough to admit your mistakes, smart enough to profit from them, and strong enough to correct them.

3. Don't repeat your mistakes. Someone once said, "There is nothing wrong with making mistakes. Just don't respond with encores." This is simple, yet profound advice. Every time we repeat a mistake, the price goes up.

Two college roommates were enjoying a late-night Western movie. As they watched a cowboy riding his horse straight toward a cliff, Jim says to his buddy, "I'll bet that guy rides over the cliff."

"He's not dumb enough to do that," Bill responded. "Twenty bucks says you're wrong."

When your watch gets out of order, you have a choice of two things to do: throw it in the fire, or take it to be fixed. The former is the quickest.

MARK TWAIN

Moments later, the cowboy and his horse headed over the cliff. Bill silently pulled 20 dollars from his billfold and handed it to Jim.

"I can't take your money," Jim responded, "I've seen the movie before."

"So have I," Bill sheepishly said, "but I didn't think the guy would do it again."

Have you ever made a mistake, recognized how stupid it was, and then turned right around and repeated the same mistake? Don't despair. You're not the only one. Repeated blunders are the fruit of habit. Some of our decisions and actions have become second nature and even failure-laden behaviors are more easily repeated than changed.

Once you break through the cycle of recurring mistakes, you create healthier habitual behavior that revolves around making the most of a situation, but being determined not to repeat it. Pearl Buck suggested, "Every great mistake has a halfway moment, a split second when it can be recalled and perhaps remedied." When you feel yourself beginning to enter the path of a familiar mistake, interrupt the journey and redirect your efforts.

Don't beat up yourself for messing up, but do admit it, learn from it, and for goodness sake, don't keep repeating it.

LIFE CAN BE A BUMMER

dversity is a natural part of life. "Most do not fully see this truth that life is difficult," wrote W. Scott Peck, in *The Road Less Traveled*. "Instead they moan more or less incessantly, noisily or subtly, about the enormity of their problems . . . as if life were generally easy, as if life SHOULD be easy." Life isn't easy. Life can be downright tough. Difficulties are as much a natural part of life as the air we breathe. Like it or not, trials and tribulations come with the territory of living. It's all a part of living in an imperfect world.

To ignore the fact, that the continual presence of adversity also applies to work, would indicate the ultimate in self-deception. You'll frequently find yourself in the middle of painful situations, perplexities, and problems, or waiting for them to reveal their ugly head. One thing is for sure: These situations will reveal the substance of which you're really made.

Setbacks can sting a little, knock you off your feet, or cause you to step back and evaluate your situation and deter-

Success is not measured by what a man accomplishes, but by the opposition he has encountered, and the courage with which he has maintained the struggle against overwhelming odds.

CHARLES
LINDBERGH

mine what you can learn. Victory comes when you accept the fact that the challenges, difficulties, and sometimes heartbreaking disappointments you experience need not ruin your life. Walt Disney once reflected, "All the adversity I've had in my life, all my troubles and obstacles have strengthened me. . . . You may not realize it when it happens, but a kick in the teeth may be the best thing in the world for you." It will probably take some considerable convincing to get us to that way of thinking. Taking small, incremental steps in that direction is a start.

Every day, multitudes of people count themselves victors over unfortunate and, sometimes seemingly unbearable, challenges. Rather than protest the inequities of their situation, which seems to be popular today, they adjust their attitudes, harness their energies, and elevate themselves to perform at a higher level. In many cases, they go on to perform far above the expected results.

Let me refresh your memory concerning a few of these people. In spite of having his first novel *(A Time to Kill)* rejected by 28 publishers, John Grisham has sold millions of copies of such books as *The Firm* and *The Client*. It takes incredible fortitude to keep on writing when 28 people have indicated they don't think much of your work. Now, every time he turns out another new book, newspapers, book reviewers, and movie producers take notice. It is now commonplace to see Grisham's name and book titles listed on the nation's bestseller lists. Grisham would probably agree with Harry Emerson Fosdick, who said: "Life does not simply ask how much can you do. It asks how much you can endure, and still be unspoiled. What a testing of character adversity is!"

Jane Pauley would concur. Being a six-time loser in the Homecoming Queen elections in school didn't keep Jane Pauley from becoming a famous television personality. Then, at the top of a seemingly perfect career, she is encouraged to make a much publicized exit from national prominence. Enough is enough, right? Not for Jane Pauley. She stepped back, refocused, and went on to help create an award-winning news show that once again allows her to excel in front of the camera.

"Show me someone who has done something worthwhile," said Lou Holtz, "and I'll show you someone who has overcome adversity." Diving champion Greg Louganis is a good example of that. He was in first place in the springboard diving preliminaries at the 1988 Summer Olympics when he hit his head on the ninth dive. Even stitches couldn't blur his focus. Instead of hanging up his trunks, Louganis maintained his concentration and executed one of the best dives of the competition. Adversity causes some people to lie down and quit, while inspiring others to reach new levels. "Adversity causes some men to break; others to break records," declared William Arthur Ward.

Franklin D. Roosevelt was paralyzed by polio at the age of 39 but didn't let the pain and disability keep him from pursuing his potential. Eight years later, he became governor of New York and, in 1932, he was elected President of the United States. Steve Palermo's successful career as an American League umpire was interrupted when he was shot coming to the aid of a robbery victim. After hundreds of hours of rehabilitation, he regained partial use of his legs and reemerged in baseball as the special assistant to the chairman of Major League Baseball's governing Executive Council. Woody Allen flunked motion picture production at New York University and the City College of New York. Even failing English didn't keep Allen from becoming an Academy Award-winning writer, producer, and director.

These men, representing diverse backgrounds and experiences, share a common bond. Life wasn't kind. Some bad things just happen (like polio), other bad things are done to us (like being shot), and some bad things can be the result of our own frailties (like flunking classes). No matter what the situation, Napoleon Hill was right. "Life is a struggle," he said, "and the rewards go to those who meet difficulty face to face, overcome it, and move on to the next challenge."

Robert Schuller suggested that "Most people who succeed in the face of seemingly impossible conditions are people who simply don't know how to quit." Take Lee Iacocca, for instance. He was on the top of his career in 1978. Iacocca had just orchestrated two record years of profit for Ford Motor Company when Henry Ford called Iacocca in his office and fired him. Within two weeks, after ending his 32-year career with Ford, Iacocca took over control of the struggling, almost bankrupt, Chrysler Corporation. In addition to dealing with being fired, he now faced a tremendous challenge to keep Chrysler alive. Iacocca pulled out all the stops, begged the government for a loan, agreed to forego a personal salary, walked the manufacturing floors to keep hope alive, and turned a major personal letdown and pending corporate tragedy into his greatest opportunity.

Vanessa Williams was forced to resign in 1984 as the first black Miss America because of a mistake she made as a teenager, posing for nude photos. One thing led to another.

She was turned down by a co-op apartment board in New York City as an "inappropriate person." Her audition for the Broadway musical *My One and Only* was vetoed by the powers-that-be. Williams persisted and made her mark as a singer with several Grammy Award nominations and landed a highly applauded starring role in *Kiss of the Spider Woman*.

Looking back on her hard knocks, Ms. Williams could surely relate to the words of Dr. Samuel Johnson when he said, "Life affords no higher pleasure than that of surmounting difficulties, passing from one step of success to another, forming new wishes and seeing them gratified."

When we look at all the achievers mentioned, and their incredible tenacity, we should draw courage and comfort from their experiences. Their stubborn refusal to allow adversity to darken their lives is a testament to our ability to deal with life's less-than-pleasurable circumstances. "History has demonstrated," observed publisher B. C. Forbes, "that the most notable winners usually encountered heartbreaking obstacles before they triumphed. They won because they refused to become discouraged by their defeats."

Maybe you have felt like the humorist who said, "When I was feeling down, someone told me, 'Cheer up, things could get worse.' So I cheered up—and they did!" "When things are bad, we take a bit of comfort in the thought that they could be worse," Malcolm Forbes comforted. "And when they are, we find hope in the thought that things are so bad they have to get better."

Take heart. The valleys of your career are inevitable. Life is simply a mixture of pleasure and pain, intended to produce maturity. They are also unpredictable. We rarely know what challenge lurks around the corner.

Adversity is not a respecter of persons. It is totally impartial. When you experience a downturn in life, it doesn't mean you are a bad person. You're human. Don't ask, "Why me?" A more suitable response is, "Why not me?" William James believed, "Acceptance of what has happened is the first step to overcoming the consequences of any misfortune."

Your disappointing times are temporary. They won't last forever and, in light of your entire career, they are short-lived. For these brief moments, there is a purpose to the pain. Henry Ward Beecher believed, "Troubles are often the tools by which God fashions us for better things." Every difficulty possesses the opportunity to change, grow, and build charac-

The important and decisive factor in life is not what happens to us, but the attitude we take toward what happens. The surest revelation of one's character is the way one bears one's suffering. Circumstances and situations may color life, but by the grace of God, we have been given the power to choose what that color shall be . . .

CHARLES R. WOODSON

ter. Each experience is a natural part of the process of shaping and molding the person you can become and preparing the way for the career success you can experience. God doesn't cause bad things to happen, but uses them to build us.

Stedham Graham suggested, "There are two ways to respond when your vision for a better life is challenged. You either give up or step up." When faced with undesirable situations, you can "step up":

1. Know exactly what you face. Get the facts.

2. Determine the worst possible outcome and how you would deal with it.

3. Determine what advantageous purpose this difficulty can serve.

4. Use the situation to learn new insights about yourself and strategies for dealing with the challenge.

5. Begin to take action that will prepare you for the worst possible outcome.

6. Refuse to feel sorry for yourself.

7. Accept full responsibility for your response.

8. Work with an unwavering spirit to meet the challenge.

9. Continually focus on how you will grow from this situation.

10. Acknowledge all of the good things in your life.

You can navigate your way through the adversities of life and refuse to give in to the impulse to quit. There will be times when your dreams are crushed and your hopes become clouded. You might feel like an utter failure or begin to question your competence. Doubt can set in, making you wonder if things will ever get better.

Norman Vincent Peale endured his fair share of adversity and yet surfaced stronger and more positive each time. He wrote, in *Enthusiasm Makes the Difference,* "Without struggle, how could a person become rounded and mature and strong? Not only are trouble and suffering inevitable, but they serve a definite creative purpose. You gradually learn to take difficulties as part of the maturing process. So when the going gets tough, take the attitude that rough spots are being knocked off. That you are being shaped for the real purpose of your life. As tough and unpleasant as difficulty may be, it is the source of potential development." The impact adversity has on your life is up to you.

ESCAPE THE BOTTOM
OF THE CAN

We must look for ways to be an active force in our own lives. We must take charge of our own destinies, design a life of substance and truly begin to live our dreams.

LES BROWN

❀

I was scheduled to conduct an all-day program entitled "Bringing Out the Best in You" at a school attempting to reach out to at-risk students. This motivational, personal development seminar was offered to all students attending the school. I arrived early in the morning to get set up and mentally prepare for the day. Then I experienced the ultimate ego-buster . . . nobody came. That's right, not one person showed up and to top it off, the seminar organizer wasn't surprised. "Even though we offer to pay students to come," he said, "they don't see the benefit in participating."

"Help me understand," I said, showing my disbelief.

"Do you fish?" my host asked.

"Only if I have to," I responded as we both chuckled.

Then he turned serious. "Imagine two fishermen sitting on a river bank next to each other, enjoying the warmth of the day and their favorite leisure activity. One fisherman is struggling to keep his crab bait in the can. The crabs keep climbing up the side of the can and the fisherman pushes them back down. He notices his fishing buddy doesn't have a problem with his bait. The crabs all sit motionless at the bottom of the can."

"How do you keep your bait from escaping?" the fisherman asked his partner.

"It's very simple," the man replied. "I have one crab who loves the bottom of the can and is offended when others try to escape. When that happens, he reaches up and pulls them back to the bottom. Eventually, they all become satisfied with their condition at the bottom of the can."

"That's a powerful story!" I said.

"It's more than a story," he immediately responded. "It's a way of life."

I stared out the windshield of my rental car on the trip back to the airport. "It's a way of life" kept ringing in my ears. That explained the continued high unemployment rate, frequency of alcoholism, history of self-destructive behaviors; not to mention a lack of interest in attending a personal development program. No matter how hard someone tried to escape, the pull to remain at the bottom of the can prevailed.

Every culture, society, community, and organization has a "bottom of the can" population who threaten to spread an epidemic of despair. The "bottom of the can" insulates people from the real world, with a false sense of security, comfort, and protection from the realities of the outside world. They remain isolated from the world's vast opportunities, richness of life, and the potential for something better by proclaiming themselves victims. Their escape is prolonged, if not averted altogether, by their unwillingness to move from passive victims to active achievers. Ultimately, their deceptive maneuvers strip themselves and those around them of positive life choices, attitudes, and actions.

When we learn to despise the "bottom of the can" mentality, we set the wheels in motion to escape destructive habits, emotional trauma, relational discourse, and the victim mentality. "The moment the slave resolves that he will no longer be a slave, his fetters fall," believed Indian nationalist and spiritual leader Mohandas Gandhi. "He frees himself and shows the way to others. Freedom and slavery are mental states." I love this final comment about freedom and slavery being mental states. Both are choices. Living at the bottom of the can is a choice.

I encourage you to live an empowered life, where you hold yourself accountable for escaping self-made prisons of misery by resisting the pull of toxic people and environments. Dr. Benjamin Elijah Mays, former president of Morehouse College, said it perfectly: "It is not your environment, it is you—the quality of your mind, the integrity of your soul, the determination of your will—that will decide your future and shape your life." Don't count on anyone else coming along to pull you out. Put yourself in charge of escape. You are the one who must see and endorse the future benefits of this self-determined lifestyle, or the motivation to take charge of your life will be lost.

The journey up the side of the can begins with you. Take the initiative and make the first move. Climb deliberately, expecting a tug to return to the bottom. Resist. Ignore those who try to discourage you. Don't give up and don't give in. This bold move takes courage, but the view and experience on the outside is well worth the effort.

On the river of life are strong currents which, left unchallenged, carry us downstream. We can either choose to be their passive victim, or we can start actively going against the flow.

KURT D. BRUNER

RETHINK WHAT
YOU THINK

*Keep your face to the sunshine, and you
cannot see the shadows.*

HELEN KELLER

ACCENTUATE THE POSITIVE

A small plant called the "sundew" grows in the Australian Bush Country. It has a slender stem and tiny round leaves fringed with hairs that glisten with bright drops of fluid. Attractive and harmless red, white, and pink blossoms adorn the plant.

Look out for the leaves, though. They are deadly. The shiny moisture on each leaf is sticky and will imprison any bug or insect that flirts with it. As the insect struggles to get free, the vibration triggers the leaves to close tightly around it. The innocent-looking plant then feeds on its victim.

The leaves of negativity: moaning, groaning, complaining, awfulizing, and self-pity appear harmless. But, they are deadly traps. They suffocate your ability to maintain an objective view of your experiences and put you on the fast track to discouragement and depression.

Have you ever known anyone who seems to be against everything? Just listen to the conversations around you. Churches, communities, organizations, and even families are

Life has, indeed, many ills, but the mind that views every object in its most cheering aspect, and every doubtful dispensation as replete with latent good, bears within itself a powerful and perpetual antidote.

LYDIA H.
SIGOURNEY

being inundated with what's wrong. No matter how positive something is, someone is there to see the dark side. Their life consists of taking the contrary view to most every issue. A mindset is created wherein they believe it is their obligation to point out life's negatives to the world. What a miserable and restrictive lifestyle. And what good does it do? Zippo. Zero. Absolutely nothing constructive.

Helen Keller's comment deserves our attention. If our minds are constantly focused on what's wrong, we'll block any sunshine in our shadow-prone world. This form of pessimistic mania is psychologically fatal and infectious. The amount of energy expended in this lifestyle is phenomenal. Accentuating the positive might require a thought transfusion and a heavy regimen of optimism to overcome current self-imposed misery, but it will be well worth whatever effort it takes.

Dan Millman, writing in *Way of the Peaceful Warrior,* said, "Your mind is your predicament. It wants to be free of change, free of pain, free of the obligations of life and death. But change is a law, and no amount of pretending will alter that reality." You have the ability to alter the impact of change. What you think about, say about, and do about change will determine your attitude toward it and your ability to deal with it. You see in every situation what you have conditioned yourself to see. The way you mentally interpret what's happening is far more important than the event itself.

How do you accentuate the positive?

- Remember your choices.

- Stay focused on purpose.

- Maintain a sense of humor.

- Look beyond the present situation.

- Accept negative emotions, deal with them, and move on.

- Eliminate negativity.

- Behave in a manner consistent with the way you want to feel.

- Create fun in your daily experiences.

Peak performers maintain a positive and productive attitude toward change. The reason is simple. By concentrating on what's going right, you boost your ability to deal with change. Accentuating the positive is a habit worth pursuing. Now, don't think this transformation can happen overnight. Be patient with yourself and those around you, but maintain an earnest commitment to begin using your energies to create new ideas, pursue dreams, and capitalize on the benefits change produces. You'll be amazed at how energized you become.

BREAK THE CHAINS

*Impossible is
a word to be
found only in
the dictionary
of fools.*

NAPOLEON
BONAPARTE

✳

Ramananda, a wiry 107-pound man from India, sat in the middle of a University of Minnesota auditorium floor on a warm August evening. Dr. O. P. Tiwari of Chicago described him to the audience. "Please don't forget Ramananda is 68. He's a medical miracle who's done 5,000 push-ups nonstop."

A chain with links of half-inch steel was brought out. "Come and try to pull it apart," Dr. Tiwari challenged the audience. Ten people, five on each end, had no effect at all.

The 6-foot chain was wrapped around Ramananda's waist, strung between his bended legs, and connected to a metal bar under his feet. "You will now see what can happen if the mind is under control," Dr. Tiwari announced.

The spindly little man, sitting on the floor, braced himself against the bar under his feet. His body tensed; then the legs plunged forward. The chain broke in the middle of a link!

My first reaction was "That's impossible!" And, for me, it probably is, not because of the chains around the body but because of the chains I place around my expectations. Charles Kettering was addressing this issue when he said, "It's amazing what ordinary people can do if they set out without preconceived notions."

Nothing ordinary or splendid is ever achieved except by those who dare to believe that their inner strength is greater than the challenge. This chain-breaking attitude opens the door to virtually unlimited opportunities.

Swimmer Susie Maroney split the chain of impossibility by completing the 112-mile swim between Cuba and the Florida Keys.

Maroney, 22, made it ashore 24-1/2 hours after leaving Havana, becoming the first woman to swim across the Florida Straits. She emerged from the surf sunburned and welted from jellyfish stings, but also with the knowledge she had done what no other woman had ever done before. "So many times you think 'I just don't want to keep going,'" she said, her tongue swollen from the salt water. "My body is aching all over."

Doug Larson once said, "Some of the world's greatest feats were accomplished by people not smart enough to know

I think it's interesting how much we can accomplish before we find out we can't do something.

GENERAL
LESLIE
GROVES

they were impossible." Maybe some of us aren't so smart as we think we are. What chains are binding you from accomplishment? What doubts and fears tend to creep into your mind whenever you consider a challenging task?

Breaking the chains isn't a matter of climbing a higher mountain, swimming a further distance, or building a bigger business. It's about conquering yourself—your hopes, your fears.

What could you do if you didn't know what you could do?

DON'T POISON THE ENVIRONMENT

Bellyachers, moaners, and groaners poison the world with their verbal pollution. It's a frustrating problem. Everybody suffers from it, many contribute to it, and only a few realize they are doing it.

Several years ago *Psychology Today* ran an article about a man who committed three hours a day, for ten years, to complaining. Each day he'd call, write, or talk to someone about what he thought was wrong with the world. Rather than changing anything, the article concluded that the only result of this exercise was that it made the man incredibly miserable.

Verbal poisoning is highly contagious, especially for people who work or live together. When you are surrounded by a professional grumbler, it's easy to get caught up in the habit. Beware of becoming one of the following environment destroyers.

- **Catastrophizers.** These people blow everything out of proportion. Little irritants become giant problems.

The poison of pessimism creates an atmosphere of wholesale negativism where nothing but the bad side of everything is emphasized.

CHARLES SWINDOLL

If one thing is wrong, everything is wrong. If one person in a department is difficult to deal with, a generalization is made that the entire department is bad. One young person with challenging behaviors is soon viewed as the entire youth population. See things as they really are, not through a misguided, tainted magnifying glass.

- **Whiners.** These people look like they were weaned on dill pickles. They wake up negative and proceed through the day making their list of why life is unfair. Sob stories, a "poor me" attitude, and helplessness make up their daily agenda. They sponsor frequent "pity parties" so others know they are undervalued and unappreciated. Whiners are the leaders in living unhappy, unfulfilled lives. Their belief that the world is out to get them and to give them a lifetime of trouble results in a prison of discontent, built with their own hands.

- **Bad Finders.** Just as it sounds, bad finders have decided their life's job description is to find everything bad in the world to them and to the people around them. Interestingly enough, these people possess an external perfectionist attitude. Why external? They believe everything and everyone outside of themselves should be perfect, but there is always something wrong.

Other people cause problems, they believe they have little or no control in their lives, and change creates insurmountable problems.

This personality is characterized by the cute story of a mother taking her son to school. As they pull up in front of the school, the little boy says, "Mommy, we didn't see any idiots today." "No, son, we didn't," mom replied. "Why did you say that?" "Yesterday, when Daddy took me to school, we saw seven idiots on the way."

- **Cynics.** Have you ever known people who are against everything? The greatest miracle in the world could occur right before their eyes and their cynical perspective would immediately take over to find a minuscule flaw. Cynics hold themselves as intellectually superior; therefore, their job is to keep the rest of us informed of what's wrong with the world. Robert Kennedy once said, "One-fifth of the people are against everything all the time." Those are the cynics. Communities, churches, organizations, and even families plagued with a cynic in their midst live with a continual burden.

People who verbally poison the environment are like the man who joined a monastery in which the monks were allowed to speak only two words every seven years. After the first seven

The thing that separates good players from great ones is mental attitude. It might only make a difference of two or three points in an entire match, but how you play those key points often makes the difference between winning and losing. If the mind is strong, you can do almost anything you want.

CHRIS EVERT

❀

years had passed, the new candidate met with his superior who asked him, "Well, what are your two words?"

"Food's bad," replied the man, who then went back to spend another seven-year period before once again meeting with the superior.

"What are your two words now?" asked the superior.

"Bed's hard," responded the man.

Seven years later the man was called to meet with the superior his third and final time.

"And what would you like to say this time?" he was asked.

"I quit."

"Well, I'm not surprised," answered the disgusted clergy. "All you've done since coming here is complain, complain, complain."

Don't be like that man, who when offered an opportunity to speak, could only find negative words to describe his experience. Contrary to popular opinion, talk is not cheap. Talk is extremely expensive. What we say powerfully affects us and those around us. Make a pact with yourself to refrain from any conversation that would pollute or poison yourself or those with whom you live, work, or socialize.

LOOK FOR THE BLUE SKY

Martin Seligman, in his book *Learned Optimism*, has developed the scientific basis for optimism. According to Seligman, you can either be pessimistic, discouraged, and helpless; or you can be optimistic, positive, courageous, and seek solutions. The choice is up to you. Nobody else is in charge of your attitude. Either way, you are responsible; and you enjoy, or pay, the consequences.

The pessimist complains about the wind; the optimist expects it to change; the realist adjusts the sails.

WILLIAM ARTHUR WARD

The Oscar-winning movie *Forrest Gump*, a top-ten all-time money-maker in Hollywood history, was an encouraging display of attitude as a choice. Even though many critics called the movie "simplistic," or "sappy," or just a "feel good" movie, I tend to think it offered much more. Maybe those who berated it in critiques are just negative, pessimistic people who felt the message hit too close to home.

Forrest Gump experiences a series of almost unimaginable, unbearable tragedies. He is born with limited intelli-

An optimist is a driver who thinks that empty space at the curb won't have a hydrant beside it.

CHANGING TIMES

❋

gence and further plagued with the need to wear leg braces. He is constantly teased and tormented by his peers.

Eventually Forrest goes to war and must face the devastating experience of having his best friend die in his arms while also watching his courageous commanding officer lose both legs on the battlefield.

The mother he adored with his life dies before his eyes; and the woman he has loved since childhood rejects him over and over again. After 20 years of diligent pursuit, Forrest wins her over, only to have her die within a few months after their marriage.

Thus far, the story line doesn't reflect a "feel-good" theme. If Forrest had been brainwashed with today's culture, he would have been expected to declare himself a victim and wallow in self-pity. Instead of whining, Forrest Gump holds fast to his endearing and unshakable optimism and frequently voices his gratitude for what he has. To him "life is like a box of chocolates; you never know what you're gonna get." But the inspiring message here is that no matter what you get, life is only as sweet or sour as you make it. Thank you, Mr. Gump.

You have a choice about what you believe, your expectations, and how you respond to life. Your choice is an accurate indicator of the person you really are. And the people and world around you ultimately reflect back what you send out.

An optimist may see a light where there is none, but why must the pessimist always run to blow it out?

MICHEL DE SAINT-PIERRE

"A pessimist is one who makes difficulties out of his opportunities," said Harry Truman. "An optimist is one who makes opportunities out of his difficulties." Optimism isn't some starry-eyed state of mind that believes the future will automatically be ideal. Instead, an optimist learns to act in a way that will create a positive future.

Evidence is building that this positive expectancy helps the optimist withstand discomfort, overcome discouragement, and turn stress into results-oriented energy and drive. Positive expectancy has also been identified with healthy self-confidence and the pursuit of dreams.

Pessimists, on the other hand, feel bad even when they feel good, for fear of how bad they will feel when they feel better. Regardless of how good things are, the pessimist is always bleak about the future. The epitaph on a pessimist's tombstone should read "I told you this would happen." Of course, "The nice part about being a pessimist," writes George Will, "is that you are constantly being either proven right or pleasantly surprised."

*Optimism is
the cheerful
frame of mind
that enables
a teakettle to
sing, though
in hot water
up to its nose.*

AUTHOR
UNKNOWN

❊

It's amazing how cartoons can drive home a point with only a few words. Such is the case from a classic "Pogo" cartoon from the 1970s. It was a simple two-frame cartoon. The setting in frame one showed Pogo standing in a mud hole, looking down at the huge mess surrounding him. The second frame showed Pogo in the same situation, but looking up at a beautiful blue sky filled with birds, a few fleecy white clouds, and a bright sun. The captions were simple:

Frame 1:   You can spend your whole life looking down at the yuck and muck and mire all around your feet, or

Frame 2:   You can look up, AND SEE THE SKY!

I recently flew from Florida back to the midwest. Weather reports indicated the midwest was socked in with bad weather. However, the 2-1/2 hours I spent flying at 30,000 feet were breathtakingly beautiful. The sky was a crisp clear blue and the sun shone with a glistening brightness. Then we started our descent into the clouds and the plane began to shake. The sun disappeared and we were engulfed in the darkness of thick gray clouds. Landing was a little tricky as the 40- to 50-mile-an-hour wind gusts made a soft landing virtually impossible. As I exited the airport, the cold rain pelted my face and I thought how ironic it was that only a few minutes earlier I was enjoying the awesome view above the clouds.

Just like the Pogo cartoon, I realized the sky is always blue. It's just a matter of where you are looking and what you are expecting to see. If in our darkest moments, the sky remains clear blue, what are you looking for?

Look for the blue sky!

STAY BALANCED

Man's last freedom is his freedom to choose
how he will react in any given situation.

VICTOR FRANKL

KEEP LIFE'S IRRITATIONS IN PERSPECTIVE

There was no reason to believe the 2-hour and 50-minute flight from Newark, New Jersey to Minneapolis, Minnesota would involve anything out of the ordinary. However, a cute little blond-haired, blue-eyed two-year-old had a different plan.

The flight was sold out and it took considerable time for me to reach my seat in the middle of the plane. As I stuffed my briefcase into the overhead compartment, a restless young flyer, unhappy at being strapped in his seat, introduced himself to his plane full of flying companions by squealing "Me Out!" "Me Out!"

I found my seat and politely introduced myself to the gentleman next to me. It was immediately apparent he was a nervous flyer and would prefer the flight be over before it started.

No sooner had I strapped myself in than I heard the little guy across the aisle in the window seat repeat his familiar

There is a technique, a knack, for thinking, just as there is for doing other things. You are not wholly at the mercy of your thoughts, any more than they are you. They are a machine you can learn to operate.

ALFRED
NORTH
WHITEHEAD

phrase, "Me Out!" Then he added a second verse: "EEE!" "EEE!" It was a shrilling and irritating sound.

By the time our 727 jet folded its landing gear and ascended into the sky, I had endured dozens of "Me Out!" "EEE!" "EEE!" combinations. Surely his mother would soon quiet her child and I could comfortably settle in for the remainder of the flight.

But such was not the case. In fact, this little guy possessed a well-established voice box that allowed him to reverberate his verbal combinations up to ten times a minute. I counted. He possessed unbelievable perseverance.

People within listening distance were becoming visibly irritated. In fact, the young man sitting next to me plugged his ears with his fingers, then buried his head in his hands and finally excused himself for an extended visit to the rear of the plane. Other travelers put pillows against their ears and several resorted to airline or personal headphones. No matter how desperately people tried, there was no escaping.

"Me Out!" "EEE!" "EEE!" "EEE!" This youngster was intent on "entertaining" us the entire flight. There were a few short-lived pauses to wet his vocal chords with apple juice. Even the airline attendants displayed their agitation by frequently visiting our area and asking the mother if there was anything they could do. She gracefully declined, holding her forefinger in front of her mouth and reminding the little boy to Shhh. Every intervention was followed by a brief mischievous smile and then, "Me Out!" "Me Out!" "EEE!" "EEE!" "EEE!" "Me Out!"

The unknown airline captain was a popular man as he taxied the plane to the gate and moved us all closer to freedom. As the seatbelt sign went off, several annoyed passengers got to their feet and immediately turned to cast a disgusting glare at their young traveling companion. I must admit, I shot a quick disapproving glance of my own, but quickly smiled, realizing what this boy had achieved.

The little guy remained unfazed. He drew a deep breath and responded to his silent but obvious critics with a final "EEE!" "EEE!" "Me Out!"

As I walked through the airport to catch my connecting flight, I marveled to myself how easily the quality of our airplane ride was tainted by one child's behavior. I was further reminded how every person's reaction was determined, not by the child's behavior, but by our reaction to it.

The events of this flight are not unlike our life encounters. No one can control the action of others or the many events of life that tend to upset us, but we can control our reactions to these behaviors and circumstances.

Your mind and thoughts are your own. You are the controller of every reaction you experience. Only you can decide the impact of your experiences. The simple truth is that you choose your perspective on life.

IT'S TIME TO DEAL WITH OVERLOAD

Look around at the number of people who are extremely busy but attaining few results. Work has become an accumulation of exhausting activity and effort. Their lives are complicated by too many commitments and not enough energy to give to them all.

Meeting mania. Memo madness. Overwhelming to-do lists. Rushing here and running there. Personal appointments. Family commitments. Confusion over responsibilities. Ringing phones. Demanding people. Unexpected crises. The list goes on and on.

A Time/CNN poll finds that more than 66 percent of us would like to "slow down and live a more relaxed life," in contrast to only 19 percent who say they would like to "live a more exciting, faster-paced life."

We've become infected with activity overload. This contagious phenomenon happens when our lives are filled to the point of being incapable of handling anything else. Without

Next week there can't be any crisis. My schedule is already full.

HENRY A. KISSINGER

appropriate action, we are on a one-way street to personal ineffectiveness. An emotional or physical "crash" is waiting just around the corner.

When the trauma of overload occurs with computers, extra disks and quick offloading are required to make the machines serviceable again. Seldom-used information is stored away, big projects receive their own disks, and old stuff is discarded. The "disk full" indicator goes off until such time as overload reoccurs. The computer breathes a sigh of relief and is off and running normally again.

Maybe it's time to evaluate your activity files. Are your energies and talents being activated in directions that leave you feeling fulfilled and satisfied with the results you achieve? Or are you in a reactive mode and hear yourself frequently lamenting:

"There just isn't enough time."

"I have too much to do and so little time to do it."

"I'm so busy."

"I can't handle any more."

There remains an enigma that seems to ignite these complicating attitudes, actions, and lifestyles. It's the mystery of balance.

Maintaining equilibrium. Juggling demands. Having a handle on what drives you. Knowing your personal limitations. Living an enabled and empowered life.

The circus tightrope walker stands on a rope high above an anxious crowd. She holds a long bar in her hands and anticipates the balance needed to make the journey to the other side. Adding to the suspense, she climbs on the seat of a unicycle she will pedal across the rope.

The professional tightrope artist knows not to begin until everything is properly aligned. Only then does she begin the slow and careful journey.

If at any time her balance waivers, she must stop to regain her composure. For the tightrope expert, balance is everything. Without it, failure and possible serious injury are certain.

Like the tightrope walker, you need balance in your life to insure a successful journey. When the pressures cause you to lose your balance, it is important to regain composure before continuing.

There are no shortcuts in the quest for balance. The right tools are important, but not enough. Getting from one end of the platform to the other is achieved by walking a

No one can maintain more than three priorities.

Most people understand this intuitively. But they keep overcommitting themselves and overcomplicating their lives. So my advice is simple: Figure out what priorities are, and say no to everything else.

ELAINE ST. JAMES

straight line determined by the final destination you've chosen. And in the midst of your busyness, stop to ask, "Am I really doing what matters most in my life?"

Reactive people will blame the environment, other people, an overwhelming workload, and a million other factors outside of themselves. Responsive, proactive people determine to take personal responsibility for the quality of their day and the extent of their productivity.

Life is not meant to be lived at breakneck speed. Such a reckless pace leads to overload and exhaustion. Yet, past experiences, the expectations of others, and our own attitudes about what we should accomplish have a tremendous influence on us.

What do you presently believe about the "musts" in your daily schedule? Are they really "have-to's"? Do they exist because you've filled your life with "shoulds" and now the only thing left to do is to save face? Oftentimes, our lives reflect the interjected demands from outside sources.

Self-imposed expectations—like being perfect, remaining strong, pleasing everyone, and a cadre of other possibilities—need to be put in perspective. Dismantle the belief that you can't get organized or that there just isn't enough time. Stop finding excuses when deadlines are missed. Quit blaming others or comparing what you are capable of achieving to the accomplishments of others.

Erase the thought that recklessly running to and fro is a noble lifestyle. Align your activities with the primary purpose in your life. Place that purpose at the top of your "to-do" list each day and remain determined to break away from doing just "to do." Your power light will come back on and you'll be energized to get involved in activities that make a difference.

ENERGIZE YOUR ABILITIES
AND KEEP LEARNING

*Your ability
needs
responsibility
to expose its
possibilities.
Do what you
can with
what you
have where
you are.*

THEODORE
ROOSEVELT

❋

The paradox of change is that people feel busier than ever, but productivity often sags. This becomes a vicious circle of busyness without results, leading to greater stress. This, in turn, creates a hesitancy to step out and try new things, and people become tentative about using their talents and abilities. The trick to making change work for you is to assess your abilities and focus on what you do best, activate your self-initiative, and get focused on results.

You've been given a gift of talents and gifts that you've never unwrapped. They are yours, but the ghastly "comfort zone" or fear of the unknown have kept you from stepping out to discover them. Now is the time for you to reevaluate and open up yourself to new possibilities.

Musician Ken Medema was born blind, but his parents made an early decision to treat him as a normal child. Ken grew up learning to play games, ride a bike, water ski, and do a host of other "normal" activities.

Ken's parents never denied his condition. They simply affirmed his worth as a human being by focusing on what he could do. Ken developed into a dynamic person with a strong inner wholeness that causes him and those around him to almost forget about his blindness.

One day on campus, Ken accidentally bumped into another blind student who said, "Hey, watch it. Don't you know I'm blind?" Instead of drawing attention to his own disability, Ken apologized. "I'm sorry. I didn't see you."

You and I are frequently bumping into situations that tend to reveal our weaknesses. The reactive approach is to use our weaknesses as excuses. Rather, acknowledge your mistakes, weaknesses, and shortcomings and then *move on.*

Discomfort is normal, but don't allow it to be an excuse for inactivity. Don't dwell on what might have been. Refrain from focusing on the negative possibilities. Focus on what you do best. Build on and sharpen your skills. Broaden the demands you place on yourself and you'll be surprised how the resources will surface to help you perform at a new level. Abilities are often hidden treasures waiting to be discovered and energized.

Surviving and thriving today might also require a certain degree of unlearning. In pursuit of an innovative, proactive lifestyle, you need to forget, ignore, and sometimes disobey the old rules, assumptions, and restrictive thoughts that have crammed our brain cells. This formidable challenge will require censoring old beliefs we've held near and dear. It is time to extinguish that which snuffs out your potential to capitalize on camouflaged opportunity. You'll be surprised how much can be discarded, eliminated, and forgotten.

Eric Hoffer said, "In a time of drastic change, it is the learners who inherit the future. The learned find themselves equipped to live in a world that no longer exists." It's no longer acceptable to be satisfied with the current level of knowledge. Build momentum by learning something new, moving forward, stretching yourself, and remaining on the cutting edge of today's demands. With your new knowledge in hand, catch a vision of what could be and relentlessly pursue it.

Numerous studies have been conducted to determine what makes a person creative. Who are those people who explore the unknown to make life meaningful? Those who create their future are optimistic. They are curious, observant, and turn innovative ideas into practical solutions.

Change-masters are open to alternatives, but retain their independent thinking. They expose themselves to new ideas and information, take the time for creatively consider-ing application, and then determine how to best turn them into assets. Their openness to new experiences allows them to take risks and not allow naysayers to hold them back. A full commitment to what they are doing makes them action-oriented people who follow their purpose and dreams.

"It is no use saying 'we are doing our best,'" Winston Churchill believed. "You have got to succeed in doing what is necessary." People who are successful today are people who believe they have much to learn, but are also confident they have much to share. They may not know exactly what the future holds for them, but they contribute to the best of their ability.

Don't focus on eliminating your weaknesses—you'll spin your wheels. Understand your abilities and put yourself in a position where they can be used. Keep learning what is needed to succeed. Combined with a responsible use of tal-ent, you'll navigate your way successfully through challenging situations.

If you want to win anything—a race, your self, your life—you have to go a little berserk."

GEORGE
SHEEHAN

GO FOR IT!

*I've felt that dissatisfaction is the basis
of progress. When we become satisfied
in business, we become obsolete.*

J. WILLARD MARRIOTT, SR.

RESIST COMPLACENCY

Mr. Marriott's comment about business has a direct correlation to people. Pablo Casals, the great cellist, was asked why, at 85 years of age, he continued to practice five hours a day. He replied, "Because I think I'm getting better." Without a fervent desire to grow, it is possible to become a victim of our own success.

Complacency can be a terrible disease that spreads throughout all areas of our life. It attacks when we're savoring our achievements and convincing ourselves that success is forever. Suddenly, we are aghast at how terrible we feel when we realize success's guarantee of longevity has run out. Failure comes knocking at the door. As Joe Paterno said, "The minute you think you've got it made, disaster is just around the corner."

Thomas Edison believed, "Restlessness is discontent—and discontent is the first necessity of progress. Show me a thoroughly satisfied man—and I will show you a failure."

The rung of a ladder was never meant to rest upon, but merely to hold a person's foot long enough to enable that individual to put the other foot somewhat higher.

THOMAS HUXLEY

Continuing hunger and restlessness is fine. I applaud it. The unguarded pursuit of more money, more recognition, increased status, peer approval, or whatever measures we use to determine success is not. These fleeting momentos of success can rapidly disappear, but living successfully can continually be renewed.

Creative discontent will forge you ahead. Stubborn selfishness impedes progress. Life needs balance.

American broadcast journalist Barbara Walters knows success. In her climb up the ladder, she commented: "Success can make you go one of two ways. It can make you a prima donna—or it can smooth the edges, take away the insecurities, let the nice things come out." This challenge for balance requires considerable effort, determination, self-discipline, and a clear understanding of what success means to us.

When success is viewed as a continuum of growth in our spiritual maturity, professional fulfillment, emotional well-being, relationship development, financial management, and mental expansion, there is little room for complacency. Based on this success paradigm, I cherish times spent with successful people. Witnessing their progress on the success journey generates excitement about the possibilities in my life. You need not, and should not, compare your achievements or life with other people, but use them as a model to elevate yourself. Notice how winners rarely back away from opportunities to grow and expand their vision. Feel the spirit that drives them toward their dreams. Pay close attention to the lifestyle of a winner and consider how you might seize the future for yourself.

Always remember, if you want to get to the top of the ladder of success, you must begin on the bottom rung. It's congested down there. In fact, one of the toughest obstacles you'll face on the way up the success continuum is the traffic jam caused by the crowds who are complacent with their growth. Don't let those people distract you. Keep climbing, growing, and reaching to become and experience everything this great life has to offer.

EXERCISE YOUR MIND

*The best
cure for a
sluggish mind
is to disturb
its routine.*

WILLIAM
DANFORTH

A team of product developers at Campbell Soup Company got together a few years ago for a brainstorming session. The group began by randomly selecting the word "handle" from a dictionary. Through free association, someone suggested the word "utensil." This led to "fork." One participant joked about a soup that could be eaten with a fork. The team reasoned that you couldn't eat soup with a fork unless it was thick with vegetables and meat—and Campbell's Chunky Soups, an extremely successful product line, was born.

There is nothing mystical about creativity. People tend to think that creativity is reserved for a select few and the rest of us will remain void of any innovative birthright. Nothing could be further from the truth. Here are a few practical ways to stimulate your creative juices. Relax. Let your mind go and enjoy the journey into creative problem solving, idea development, or product ingenuity.

1. Think fresh. R. Buckminster Fuller was a man of many talents. His adult life was spent as an inventor, engineer, architect, poet, and star-gazer. "Bucky," as his friends referred to him, was most importantly a creative thinker. He was responsible for the invention, development, and implementation of over 170 patented ideas. He authored 24 books and made 57 trips around the world sharing his abundant supply of ideas with others.

As a young nonconforming student, Fuller was expelled from Harvard in his freshman year. His enthusiasm and creativity remained undampened. Fuller would spend up to 22 hours a day studying math, architecture, and physics. His self-attained knowledge, combined with his creative ideas, made him a man ahead of his time and the leading innovator of futuristic products. In fact, he was often branded an eccentric because his ideas seemed so impossible at the time. However, the putdowns and criticism had little effect on Bucky and he continued to create, design, and invent up until his death.

R. Buckminster Fuller became one of the greatest innovators of the 20th century. His creative genius stemmed from this simple yet profound thought: "People should think things out fresh and not just accept conventional terms and the conventional way of doing things."

Murray Spangler developed a mindset recommended by Bucky Fuller. As a department store janitor, Spangler suffered considerable discomfort from the dust his broom stirred. The wheezing and coughing prompted him to find an "unconventional" way to clean floors.

"Why not eliminate the sweeping," he thought, "and suck up the dust instead." His friend, H.W. Hoover, financed the first awkward but functional vacuum cleaner. Spangler's futuristic, uncluttered thinking allowed him to overcome personal discomfort and go beyond conventional thinking.

Unconventional thinkers, people who exercise their brains, tend to stumble onto great discoveries in their pursuit of unique ideas. In 1953, a rocket chemical company chemist persisted in developing a water-displacement formula. On his fortieth attempt, he was successful in creating a substance used in 79 percent of American homes.

According to *USA Today,* the product is used to loosen toes stuck in bathtub faucets; cure mange in dogs; get stuck fingers out of soda bottles; make fish bait more attractive; loosen rusted nuts and bolts; get a burglar out of a vent pipe;

quiet squeaking wheels and springs; loosen arthritic knees and elbows.

The product? Think about it. Water displacement. 40 attempts. It's WD-40®. The famous blue-and-yellow can contains a product that comes in handy in a multitude of unconventional emergencies.

2. Expand your current thinking. Pablo Picasso endorsed a revolutionary approach to creativity. He was standing outside his house one day looking around the yard. A rusty old bicycle resting against the porch caught his attention. Picasso focused on the metal frame of the bike and noticed the handlebars resembled the horns of a bull. Removing the handlebars from the bike, he proceeded to his studio and created a sculpture of a charging bull. Picasso tapped his creative imagination to turn the ordinary into something dramatic. Picasso's creative success was attributed to the ability of expanding on one theme to create another.

Later in his life, Picasso shared the secret for escaping tunnel vision. "Every act of creation is first of all an act of destruction," preached Picasso. One must first break down the barriers of present limitations and restrictive thoughts,

Some painters transform the sun into a yellow spot; others transform a yellow spot into the sun.

PABLO PICASSO

and destroy old habits that strangle our creative efforts. Then and only then can our creative genius be explored.

3. Challenge established rules. Creativity expert Roger Von Oech says, "Challenging the established rules is necessary to awaken our creativity." Von Oech tells how in the winter of 333 B.C., the Macedonian general Alexander and his army arrived in the Asian city of Gordium to spend the winter. Alexander is told about the legend surrounding the town's famous knot, the "Gordian Knot." According to local prophecy, whoever is able to untie this exceptionally complex knot will become king of Asia. Alexander is fascinated by the local legend and asks to be shown the knot so he can attempt to untie it. He studies the strangely tied rope and makes numerous fruitless attempts to locate the rope's end.

Unscathed by his failure to unfasten the knot, he approached the challenge using Picasso's advice. Alexander pulled out his sword and sliced the knot in half . . . thereby inheriting control of Asia.

4. Get crazy. Creative people are constantly on the lookout for breakthrough ideas. They recreate and rearrange the present by finding novel ways to approach specific problems. They use their creativity to find new solutions (sometimes by using unrelated ideas as they fit the present situation). Many times the seemingly craziest ideas become the most successful. While this approach tends to invite criticism, creative thinkers continue to think things out fresh, knowing that novel ideas often solve complex problems.

Novel ideas will produce criticism from the masses, but Everett M. Rogers suggests that "When five percent of society accepts an idea, it becomes imbedded in the population. When 20 percent agrees, it's unstoppable." Even the unstoppable get criticized.

"You can't put an alligator on a shirt to replace the pocket. Nobody will buy them!"

"You want to sell me a chicken recipe? You'll never get this idea off the ground, Colonel Sanders!"

"Mr. Bell, please remove that silly toy from my office. There is no room in the market for a telephone."

"How dumb do you think I am? You can't put music on Scotch tape."

The history books are full of people who realized creativity begins with destroying perceived limitations and remaining untouched by criticism.

5. Search for new possibilities. Albert Einstein represented the best of creative thinkers when he observed, "To raise new questions, new possibilities, to regard old problems from a new angle requires creative imagination." Creativity emerges out of personal commitment to raise new questions, explore new possibilities, focus on old problems from a new angle, and be willing to implement ideas that may not be in tune with the normally accepted way of doing things.

Charles Darrow was a salesperson living during the Great Depression who must have been an advocate of Einstein's thinking. When the sales positions ceased, he squeezed out a living walking dogs, washing cars, and other assorted odd jobs. In the evening, he worked on developing a board game that several people could play at once. Darrow had visions of every home owning one of his games.

The first company to purchase his idea sold 5,000 games in the first year. Parker Brothers later purchased the game, beefed up the marketing, and today, 20,000 of these games are sold every week.

Darrow's willingness to pursue new possibilities resulted in America's favorite board game—*Monopoly*®.

What about the young salesperson asked by the Hookless Fastener Company how to increase the sale of zippers? He suggested they replace the buttons on the front of men's pants with zippers. This unconventional idea was almost scrapped. A trial run took this nontraditional idea from skepticism to a standard in the clothing industry.

A discussion on new possibilities from fresh thinking wouldn't be complete without considering George de Mestral. While brushing burrs out of his wool pants and his dog's coat, de Mestral became curious about the tenacity of the burrs. Concentrated observation of the burrs under a microscope revealed hundreds of tiny hooks snagged in mats of wool and fur. Years later, he made a connection and the invention of Velcro® fasteners was born. George de Mestral considered an old problem with new eyes. He raised new questions and sought new possibilities. Einstein would have been proud.

Dr. Michael LeBoeuf advises, "Don't let other people define your creative potential. No one, including you, knows what you're capable of doing or thinking up."

In a three-month creativity study, psychologists researched the characteristics of creative people. Education, family backgrounds, and a variety of personal preferences were all considered as possible variables. In the end, one single common factor was found to determine an individual's creativity—attitude. Simply stated, creative people think they are creative.

Creative potential is one of the great God-given tools available to us. The extent to which we develop this gift depends on our attitude towards it. No one knows for sure what he or she is capable of and therein lies the excitement.

Innovators don't always invent new radical ideas. Instead, they are careful observers of the world around them. They borrow and rethink existing ideas to solve problems and create unexposed opportunities. Nurture originality and new frontiers will be discovered.

CREATIVE PROBLEM SOLVING

A high school janitor was becoming increasingly frustrated with a group of mischievous girls who, after putting on their lipstick, would press their lips against the bathroom mirrors. By mid-morning, every day, lip prints adorned all the bathroom mirrors.

The janitor expressed his irritation with the principal who decided on a novel demonstration to discourage the continuation of this behavior. She assembled the girls in the bathroom and met them there with the custodian. She explained the inappropriateness of their behavior and pointed out the extra work they were causing the custodian. To demonstrate how difficult it was to clean off the lipstick, she asked the custodian to show the girls what he needed to do to clean the mirrors.

He pulled a long-handled brush out of his cleaning bucket, dipped it into the nearest toilet, and scrubbed the mirror.

This school's mirrors have remained free from lipstick prints.

We should always have in our heads one free and open corner, where we can give place, or lodging as they pass, to the ideas of our friends. It really becomes unbearable to converse with men whose brains are divided up into well-filled pigeon-holes, where nothing can enter from the outside.

JOSEPH
TOUBERT

SUCCESS IS JUST AROUND
THE CORNER

*Never give up
then, for
that is just
the place
and time
that the tide
will turn.*

HARRIET
BEECHER
STOWE

❀

Walter Payton is considered one of the greatest professional running backs of all time. During a Monday night football game between the New York Giants and Chicago Bears, the announcers were showering Payton with accolades. "Just think," one announcer observed, "he has accumulated over nine miles in career rushing yardage." Another announcer quickly responded, "Yeah, and that's with someone knocking him down every 4.6 yards!"

"In life or in football," Rush Limbaugh observed, "touchdowns rarely take place in 70-yard increments. Usually it's three yards and a cloud of dust." Walter Payton, an unquestionably successful running back, has raised a few clouds of dust. He knows that everyone—even the best— gets knocked down. The key to success is to get up and run harder the next time. It's called perseverance, tenacity, courage.

Tenacity is that wonderful quality that keeps writers writing, artists painting, athletes competing, the rest of us keeping on keeping on. Successful people persevere even when they are told they will never make it. Malcolm Forbes, who was editor-in-chief of *Forbes* magazine and one of the wealthiest people in America, didn't make the staff of his college paper when he was a student at Princeton.

Walt Disney had a dream that would alter the entertainment industry. He went bankrupt two or three times, had equipment repossessed, experienced a nervous breakdown, and begged for additional dollars until finally things smoothed out for him in the late 1960s. Imbedded in every Disney creation is a history of incredible tenacity and perseverance displayed by Walt Disney in the face of disheartening calamities. Maybe he had heard the words of singer Ella Fitzgerald. "Just don't give up trying to do what you really want to do. Where there is love and inspiration, I don't think you can go wrong."

Your level of persistence in the midst of difficulty, obstacles, and adversity is an accurate gauge of your belief in yourself. Successful people understand the necessity of coming face to face with life's undesirable situations, reaching deep inside, gathering their confidence and unhesitantly stepping forward. They do not give in, period. There is no second-guessing. They understand the journey will produce mental and physical fatigue, but they are not about to surrender. In fact, they fully expect to pay a handsome price for the achievements they attain. In a book of letters to his young adult son called *Mark My Words,* Canadian businessman G. Kingsley Ward writes: "No one I know of has ever experienced one success after another without defeats, failures, and disappointments, and frustrations galore along the way. Learning to overcome these times of agony is what separates the winners from the losers."

This particular man wanted to be a writer, yet he spent much of his time in the U.S. Navy writing tedious reports and letters. That wasn't the type of writing he had in mind, but such responsibilities did help refine his written communication skills. After serving his country, he kept writing and writing and writing, but experienced rejection upon rejection. Maybe becoming a published author just wasn't meant to be. Then came a little different rejection, not the normal form letter, but an encouraging note from an editor that said "Nice try."

That simple note reinsured this struggling writer and offered what he viewed as a ray of hope. Finally, after many persistent years, he penned a book that has richly affected the world. The now-world-famous author of whom I speak is Alex Haley, and his book *Roots* was also made into a television miniseries enjoyed by millions.

"Hold your head high, stick your chest out," said Reverend Jesse Jackson. "You can make it. It gets dark sometimes but morning comes." Morning does come and success is normally just around the corner. If only people wouldn't stop in the middle of Adversity Street to lament their condition. Success is waiting, but it only greets the persistent traveler.

Persistence is what makes the impossible possible, the possible likely, and likely definite.

ROBERT HALF

WHAT'S YOUR SECRET,
MR. SMITH?

Here is the test to find whether your mission on Earth is finished. If you're alive, it isn't.

RICHARD BACH

❋

Willard Scott of the "Today Show" had a memorable interview one morning with a Mr. Smith, who was celebrating his 102nd birthday. Unique to this interview were the props that accompanied Mr. Smith. Willard was having a difficult time getting Mr. Smith to focus on the interview instead of the potted chrysanthemums and orchids that surrounded him.

"Mr. Smith," Willard repeated, "we'd all like to know to what you attribute your long life." Mr. Smith, sharp as a tack, continued to draw attention to his flowers. "This little lovely won't bloom for another two years," he informed the television viewing audience. As Mr. Smith touched the flowers, sprayed them with water and gazed upon their beauty, Willard made another attempt to discover the man's secret for living 102 years. "What's your secret for living so long and staying alive?"

The old man quickly replied with a question of his own: "Who would take care of these beautiful flowers?" This wasn't exactly what Willard Scott was looking for, but Mr. Smith communicated a powerful message.

Richard Gaylord Briley suggested, "If all you do is react to what this unpredictable, irrational world throws at you, lacking positive plans and purposes of your own to give direction to your life, your life has no rational purpose beyond mere survival." The 102-year-old Mr. Smith was more interested in the purpose that provided passion in his life than the mere fact that he had "survived" for more than a century. He had learned how to put life in his living rather than just adding years to his life.

Don't make this philosophical. Present in each of us is a reason for living waiting to be discovered. To be committed and working for a valuable purpose, a purpose larger than your self-interests, is one of the secrets of making life significant. Identifying and aligning with a purpose adds meaning, stability, and direction to life.

I often think about an experience Supreme Court Justice Oliver Wendell Holmes had preparing to board a train. Apparently, Holmes had misplaced his ticket and was desperately searching to find it to avoid missing his train. The conductor sensed Holmes's frustration and said, "Your

Honor, if you do not find your ticket, you can simply mail it to the railroad. We know and trust you."

Holmes quickly replied, "I am not so concerned about your getting my ticket. I just want to know where I am going." There are a lot of people wanting to know where they are going in life.

Purposeless people are like the jaçana, a unique tropical bird. It has spindly legs with long protruding toes enabling it to skip along floating weeds or stroll across lily pads. Bird enthusiasts commonly refer to the jaçana as a "lily-trotter." Here's a bird capable of soaring through the skies that has settled for lazily moving from flower to flower.

What a waste! Yet, there are people who drift along through life skipping from one thing to the next. They've not yet realized there are fabulous adventures and new heights waiting for them to experience once they leave their "lily-trotter" existence.

If you were to look back on your wonderful, fantastic life, what would have made it so great? What does your life stand for? What is the "why" of your life? What makes living worthwhile and meaningful regardless of the challenges you experience?

George Bernard Shaw shared this reflection: "This is the true joy in life, being used for a purpose recognized by yourself as a mighty one. Being a force of nature instead of feverish, selfish little clod of ailments and grievances complaining that the world will not devote itself to making you happy. I am of the opinion that my life belongs to the whole community and as I live it is my privilege—my privilege to do for it whatever I can. I want to be thoroughly used up when I die, for the harder I work the more I love. I rejoice in life for its own sake. Life is no brief candle to me; it is a sort of splendid torch which I've got a hold of for the moment and I want to make it burn as brightly as possible before handing it on to future generations."

No individual has any right to come into the world and go out of it without leaving behind him distinct and legitimate reasons for having passed through it.

GEORGE
WASHINGTON
CARVER

IT COULD BE WORSE

*If life were predictable, it would cease to be
life and would be without flavor.*

ELEANOR ROOSEVELT

LEARN TO EXPECT (AND ENJOY) THE UNEXPECTED

Have you ever noticed how profound the "Peanuts" cartoon can be? I love the one where Charlie Brown, in the first panel, says, "I learned something in school today. I signed up for folk guitar, computer programming, stained glass, art, shoemaking, and a natural foods workshop."

The second panel has him saying, "I got spelling, history, arithmetic, and two study periods."

The third panel has his companion asking, "So, what did you learn?"

Charlie Brown offers a practical life lesson in the final panel. "I learned that what you sign up for, and what you get are two different things."

How many times have you heard someone say, "Life isn't fair. I signed up for success, happiness, and fulfillment and got challenges, disappointment, and failure. It's just not fair!"

You have to look at each day as a new opportunity to change one thing about your life.

RICK PITINO

Life is unpredictable. There is no short-order cook at our beck and call to insure everything we order is served just as we like it. Sometimes we take what's been served and make the most of it. As someone once said, "The real enjoyment of living, like the real enjoyment of eating a steak, comes when you put your teeth into it."

If life is going to be unpredictable, then what can we do about it? Good question. Some people just give up. They entertain the attitude that "What will be, will be," thereby eliminating any effort to change or mold what's happening to them. Resigning yourself to the belief there's nothing you can do to improve your life is certainly not advisable.

How about altering your expectations? The reality is some people have a tendency to expect life to bring them whatever they want, when they want it. Those who are willing to adjust this thinking endorse the insight of Kathleen Norris, that "Life is easier to take than you'd think: All that is necessary is to accept the impossible, do without the indispensable, and bear the intolerables."

I'm partial to another alternative. Madeleine L'Engle said, "When we stop waking up in the morning as though each day was going to be full of adventure, joys, and dangers, and wake up instead to the alarm clock and the daily grind, and mutter about TGIF, we lose the newborn quality of belief which is so lovely in a child." Approach the unpredictable with wonderment. Sustain the childlike curiosity and fascination with everything you encounter. Expect the unexpected. Enjoy it.

This approach runs contrary to public opinion. The majority of us would agree with George Gissing, writing in *The Private Papers of Henry Ryecroft*. He asserted: "It is familiarity with life that makes time speed quickly. When every day is a step in the unknown—as for children—the days are long with gathering of experience."

He might be right, but consider this: By increasing our exposure to the unfamiliar, we increase our repertoire of the familiar. How can we ever increase our comfort with the unfamiliar unless we increase our exposure to the uncomfortable? Those who lay down and surrender, run or fight that which bothers them, will live in a continual state of anxiety. Limited experiences create a limited life. If you want to expand the quality of your life, put out the welcome mat for unexpected visitors and enjoy their visit. "Whatever the ups and downs of detail within our limited experience," said

Gregory Bateson, "the larger whole is primarily beautiful." That's true, unless, of course, we decide to lament the ups and downs while failing to enjoy the larger whole.

If you are waiting to live life until everything happens the way you want it to, good luck.

Develop an increased tolerance for unpredictable events to interrupt your master plan, to modify your course direction, and to spring surprises on you. Give an accepting nod to increased confusion and seemingly pointless changes. We can always use what life has to offer by proactively pursuing the stockpile of possibilities. Think of your life as having movable walls that adjust to fit current demands rather than fixed walls that fracture when pressured.

Life is not predictable, in the sense that it brings you whatever you want, whenever you want it. But to those willing to expand the dimensions of their living, life will predictably produce unanticipated experiences to add richness to your living.

HANG ON THROUGH
TURBULENT TIMES

I hesitate to overpromote the benefits of adversity, but here's an observation worth your reflection. Problems produce miracles. It's true. Countless people endured more than they ever thought possible. Others in difficult situations encounter unexpected benefits. Renewed strength is experienced through the process of encouraging and working through daily challenges.

A life without difficulties, like earth exposed to constant sunshine without rain, becomes a barren desert. A life mixed with pleasure and pain produces miracles and maturity. Life needs both good and bad to be purposeful. If you're presently enduring a difficult time, prepare for a miracle.

Problems are also a primary source for discovering opportunity. Every form of trial reveals needs, and needs sensitize us to previously unexposed opportunities. Don't overlook them by being distracted with the problem or deceived by the seemingly insurmountable consequences.

Life is a series of problems. To confront them is often painful; yet it is only through solving problems that we grow . . . and give meaning to our lives. Many of us try to avoid our problems and the emotional suffering they involve, and this tendency is the primary basis of all mental illness.

M. SCOTT
PECK, M.D.

Rather, fine-tune your vision. Problems are only opportunities disguised by discomfort.

One conclusion is easily made as I observe people from all walks of life. The difference between an overwhelming problem and an opportunity is simply the person's perception of the situation. As philosopher Mafu so aptly stated, "If one's primary focus is on the manure pile, he or she will ultimately turn over flowers that 'get in the way' because one is only looking for the manure."

On a recent visit to the South, I learned that years ago farmers in southern Alabama were accustomed to planting one crop every year—cotton. They would plow as much ground as they could and plant their crop. Year after year, they thrived on cotton.

Then one year the dreaded boll weevil devastated the whole area. So the next year the farmers, intent on maintaining their livelihood, mortgaged their homes and planted cotton again, hoping for a good harvest. But as the cotton began to grow, the insects returned, infesting and destroying the crop, wiping out most of the farms.

The few who survived those two years of the boll weevil decided to experiment the third year, so they planted something they'd never planted before—peanuts. Peanuts proved hardy and a wide-open market proved so profitable that the farmers who survived the first two years reaped income that third year that enabled them to pay off all their debts. Peanuts became the crop of choice and farmers prospered with the product of adversity.

Then you know what those farmers did? They spent some of their new wealth to erect in the town square a monument—to the boll weevil. The inscription of the monument reads: "In profound appreciation of the boll weevil and what it has done to herald prosperity." If it hadn't been for the boll weevil, they never would have discovered peanuts. They learned that out of disaster, a new profitable opportunity can be discovered.

Inside of every problem is an opportunity waiting to be discovered. Once the blinders of blaming, defensiveness, negative attitudes, and self-pity are removed, intimidating situations can be broken down bit by bit to unveil positive solutions.

I'm not suggesting we ignore our problems. Quite the contrary. Face them head on. Be honest about the possible ramifications. See the circumstances as they really are—just circumstances. Face up to the tendency to respond negatively and dispel all temptation to dwell on the negative. Get a grip on your feelings and act in a way that will propel you toward discovering all the good that can result from your present situation.

I was recently told about a commuter flight from Portland, Maine to Boston. During this uneventful flight, Henry Dempsey, the pilot, suddenly heard an unusual noise coming from the rear of the aircraft. He turned over the controls of the aircraft to his co-pilot and made his way to the back to check out the mysterious sound.

As he reached the tail section, the plane encountered an air pocket and Dempsey was thrust against the rear door. He quickly discovered the reason for the mysterious noise. The rear door was inadvertently left partially unlatched prior to takeoff. The door flew open and Dempsey was sucked from the airplane's cabin out of the jet.

The co-pilot immediately saw the red light indicating an open door. He radioed the nearest airport informing them of his dilemma and requested an emergency landing. He told the air traffic controller that the pilot had fallen out of the plane and requested emergency personnel search the ocean below.

After the plane landed, Henry Dempsey was found holding onto the ladder of the aircraft. He had miraculously caught the ladder, held on for ten minutes as the plane flew 200 mph at an altitude of 4,000 feet, and then during the landing, kept his head from hitting the runway only 12 inches below. Once safely on the ground, it took airport personnel several minutes to pry Dempsey from the ladder.

Holding on can be difficult when times are tough. In fact, you might have experienced turbulence when letting go and giving up seemed the easiest thing to do. Winners are the people who keep on keeping on when the easy way out would be to get off. Henry Dempsey is proof that the best approach is to hang on for dear life until safety is reached.

The next time life deals you a nasty blow, your dreams go up in smoke, or unexpected tragedy strikes, it's time to push the reset button. Make new plans. Dream new dreams. Resist the temptation to run away, hide, give up, or cash it in. You are in line to make amazing discoveries about yourself and life. Propel yourself forward by establishing positive and fresh expectations.

I can assure you there will be turbulence ahead. Adversity is a given. Disappointment is a normal experience. But defeat need not be the end result. You have at your disposal the intestinal fortitude to hang on until a safe landing can be maneuvered.

When things are bad we take a bit of comfort in the thought that they could be worse. And when they are, we find hope in the thought that things are so bad they have to get better.

MALCOLM
FORBES

RECOGNIZE THE VALUE
OF CATFISH

*People are
like tea bags.
You never know
how strong
they are until
they're in hot
water.*

RITA MAE
BROWN

hile in the wilderness, Jesus was clearly tempted by Satan to misuse his power. When Satan said, "Worship me and you will own the world," Jesus said, "No thanks." Then Satan used a little different approach. "Satisfy your hunger, and turn these stones into bread." Again, Jesus calmly replied, "No."

"Throw yourself off the pinnacle of the temple," Satan tempted, "and test your power to spring back to eternal life." Jesus looked Satan square in the face and said, "No." (Sometimes I think Jesus should have asked Satan, "What part of NO don't you understand?")

Anyway, after 40 days of being tested in that desert, Jesus emerged with a renewed understanding of who He was and what His purpose was intended to be.

Adversity tends to reveal our true character. William Penn saw it this way: "No pain, no palm; no thorns, no throne;

no gall, no glory; no cross, no crown." The refining process of adversity prepares us for the victories to follow.

Charles Swindoll uses a story about codfish to simplify this principle. Codfish became a popular choice of many in New England and the demand for the fish spread nationwide. The problem occurs in shipping them throughout the country. At first, the transport companies tried freezing the cod, but that diminished the flavor of the fish. Then they tried shipping them alive in tanks of seawater, but they lost their flavor and also became soft and mushy.

An original thinker offered a clever solution. The cod were placed in seawater along with their natural sea-loving enemy—the catfish. Imagine this picture. During shipment the catfish chased the cod around the tank. A little game of tag, if you will, and when they arrived at their destination, the cod were as fresh as those consumed by New Englanders. There was no loss of flavor or texture.

Imagine the adversity in your life as the "catfish" appointed to keep you fresh, active, growing, and in the continual process of perfecting your character. Then we, like Jesus, when emerging from the desert can declare "I Am."

Life does not have to be perfect to be wonderful.

ANNETTE FUNICELLO

Eleanor Roosevelt once said about encountering adversity: "I gain strength, courage, and confidence by every experience in which I must stop and look fear in the face. I say to myself, 'I've lived through this and can take the next thing that comes along.' We must do the things we think we cannot do."

I don't necessarily care for the "catfish" in my life, but I'm beginning to appreciate their purpose and significance.

BREAK THROUGH THE BRICK WALL OF ADVERSITY

She held the audience in the palm of her hand. Two thousand people were captivated by her vibrant personality, distinguished stage presence, and the power of her message. Hardly an eye focused on the wheelchair or the disability that made it necessary. All eyes, ears, and hearts were endeared by the person and her challenge to capitalize on our God-given abilities even though our disabilities are more easily spotted.

Joni Eareckson Tada was paralyzed from the shoulders down as a result of a diving accident at the age of 17. Through the struggles that ensued, Joni was led to allow God to use her adversity to minister to others with disabilities and their families.

Joni is an internationally recognized artist (which she accomplished by holding a brush or pencil in her mouth), author, lecturer, and musician. Her ministry and talents have helped the world to understand that disabilities are merely challenges to be met and mastered with the grace of God.

Success is not measured by what a man accomplishes, but by the opposition he has encountered, and the courage with which he has maintained the struggle against overwhelming odds.

CHARLES
LINDBERGH

"We can decide to let our trials crush us," wrote Helen Keller, "or we can convert them to new forces of good."

Joni's new forces of good have extended into eastern and western Europe, Asia, and other places throughout the world. She epitomizes one who learned to transform a physical adversity into a blessing and challenge for all those who encounter her talents.

Facing our difficulties head on can be the springboard for building personal effectiveness. As Joni found, without her disability, she might have never found her deeper talents. She decided to use them rather than succumb to the adversity she encountered.

Dr. Michael LeBoeuf believes, "Adversity is an experience, not a final act."

On the last day of the 1979 spring baseball exhibition season, Steve Kemp, left fielder for the Detroit Tigers, took a pitch to the head and was rushed to the hospital.

Would this feared event minimize Kemp's effectiveness at the plate? Would the nightmare of that disastrous pitch haunt him every time at bat? Only time would tell.

Kemp stepped to the plate with confidence on opening day of the regular season. His first at-bat yielded a single, and a home run followed at his next time at bat. The questions had been answered.

During a post-game interview, Kemp commented, "After I was hit, I just told myself, 'I can't let it bother me. . . . If you let it bother you, you're not going to be any good to yourself or your team.'"

The brick wall of adversity blocks the road to achievement when viewed as an unconquerable barrier with lifelong consequences. Nothing can be further from the truth. A tragedy can be transformed into a triumph when viewed as a temporary roadblock (not a permanent condition).

It could be said that only those who persist through challenges can expect to rise to new heights. Mountains are designed to spur us on to loftier heights.

Bible teacher Warren Wiersbe tells the story of a little boy who was leading his younger sister up a steep mountain path. The climbing was difficult, for there were many rocks in the way. Finally, the little girl, exasperated by the hard climb, said to her brother, "This isn't a path at all. It's all rocky and bumpy." "Sure," her brother replied, "but the bumps are what you climb on."

In his book *Enthusiasm Makes the Difference,* Norman Vincent Peale offered these encouraging words: "Without struggle, how could a person become rounded and mature and strong? Not only are trouble and suffering inevitable, but they serve a definite creative purpose. You gradually learn to take difficulties as part of the maturing process. So when the going gets tough, take the attitude that rough spots are being knocked off. That you are being shaped for the real purpose of your life. As tough and unpleasant as difficulty may be, it is the source of potential development."

A life void of difficulties would reduce all possibilities to zero. Eliminate challenges, and the tension needed to produce would be nonexistent. We all have a tendency to want to eliminate problems, but they await our willingness to conquer.

Life can be a struggle. The rewards are reserved for those who meet difficulties head on, work through and overcome them, and then move on to the next challenge. Through it all comes the realization that success is achieved only through struggle. There is no shortcut. The worthwhile achievements in your life are the result of courageously negotiating struggles. You'll become only as big as the problem that stops you.

You gotta play the hand that's dealt you. There may be pain in that hand, but you play it. And I've played it.

JAMES BRADY

LIVE TO LEARN AND
LEARN TO LIVE

*Growing and learning are healthy,
normal experiences. Both have to do with
a process . . . and that process is sometimes
painful, often slow, and occasionally
downright awful! It's like taking three steps
forward and two steps back.*

CHARLES R. SWINDOLL,
Three Steps Forward, Two Steps Back

NO COASTING ALLOWED

Fast food. Ten-minute oil change. Instant cash. Quick photo processing. Express lane checkout. One-hour dry cleaning. Today's lifestyles are saturated with instant everything. Life comes at us like a bolt of lightning these days—fast, without warning. But the speed of life contains amazing possibilities for people who are prepared.

There are two kinds of people: the ones who have to be told and the ones who figure it out all by themselves.

TOM CLANCY

Charles Swindoll's observation that growing and learning is often like taking three steps forward and two steps back provides an accurate visual image of the difficulty in keeping up. You can't do everything as fast as the world is moving. The quest for success requires you to carefully choose your three steps forward based on what is most necessary for you to keep up. Then push yourself intently in that direction. One thing is sure: Coasting isn't an option.

Instead of dillydallying around, spreading yourself too thin, attempting to be everything to everybody, determine what priorities will get your attention. Carefully examine your job. Which responsibilities produce the greatest results? Begin here and start identifying ways to continuously improve. You'll achieve more impressive results by becoming 10 percent better in ten areas than 100 percent better in one area or 1 percent better in 100 areas.

We need to invest continually in personal growth to remain a well-rounded, effective, cutting-edge professional. How many books have you read in the past year? Have you listened to any good learning audiotapes recently? How many professional journals, educational magazines, or Internet learning services do you consistently peruse? How many seminars or classes have you attended since graduation? Do you have a mentor to encourage you, challenge you, and provide guidance for your growth? When you commit yourself to a regimen of accelerated growth, your odds for survival, satisfaction, and success improve.

The level of skill that helped you get where you are will not be sufficient to move you into the future. Even 10, 20, or 30 years of experience is no guarantee that you'll continue to deliver the goods the world has come to expect. Your rate of growth must equal or exceed the rate of change. Investing in spiritual, financial, social, mental, physical, family, and career development is a prerequisite for releasing your potential and adding value to your organization.

Cullen Hightower suggested, "The human body was designed to walk, run or stop; it wasn't built for coasting." That's good to know, because continual movement and improvement is today's universal modus operandi. Become a little bit better today than you were yesterday. Keep moving. Keep stretching. It puts you one step closer to your potential and prepared for today's lightning-speed changes.

GET CURIOUS

*Only the
curious will
learn and only
the resolute
overcome the
obstacles to
learning. The
quest quotient
has always
excited me
more than the
intelligence
quotient.*

EUGENE S.
WILSON

Continual learning doesn't occur by chance. You must diligently pursue it. Curiosity is a human quality that affords you valuable opportunities. William A. Ward believed: "Curiosity is the wick in the candle of learning." I guess it could be said then that without curiosity, the learning candle is rendered virtually nonexistent.

To the interested person, life experiences are packaged with innumerable possibilities for expanding knowledge. Your mind must be placed in the learning mode to take advantage of these situations.

Portia Nelson wrote a piece entitled "Autobiography in Five Short Chapters." It reads:

•   Chapter 1—I walk down the street. There is a deep hole in the sidewalk. I fall in. I am lost. . . . I am helpless. It isn't my fault. It takes forever to find a way out.

- Chapter 2—I walk down the same street. There is a deep hole in the sidewalk. I pretend I don't see it. I fall in again. I can't believe I am in the same place, but it isn't my fault. It still takes a long time to get out.

- Chapter 3—I walk down the street. There is a deep hole in the sidewalk. I see it is there. I still fall in. . . . It's a habit. My eyes are open. I know where I am. It is my fault. I get out immediately.

- Chapter 4—I walk down the same street. There is a deep hole in the sidewalk. I walk around it.

- Chapter 5—I walk down another street.

Poet Archibald MacLeish once said, "There is only one thing more painful than learning from experience, and that is not learning from experience."

How many experiences do you repeat every day without ever asking "Why am I doing this?" What habitual ways of doing things restrict you from escaping your learning comfort zone? What holes do you repeatedly fall in because you've not considered taking another street?

If you want to expand the dimensions of your life, there must be an insatiable desire to not only expand your experiences, but allow your suppressed curiosity to find out more.

Traveling as a professional speaker provides ample opportunities for me to expand my curiosity. As the ever-profound Yogi Berra once said, "You can observe a lot just by watching." Watching has become one of my favorite forms of entertainment and source of interesting learning. Some of the things I'm curious about aren't necessarily significant, but they do keep my mind churning, thinking, and exploring.

For instance, why don't airplane manufacturers build airplanes from the same material they build the infamous "black box"? Why is the back seat in 80 percent of our nation's taxis as hard as a rock? Why do cars have spare tires but no spare batteries or even a spare fan belt? Who comes up with the crazy savings on airline barf bags?

As a father of two children, I asked a question repeatedly during the Christmas season. Why don't toy manufacturers include batteries with their toys? Another favorite: Who decided 80 percent of children's toys should come unassembled?

Driving down the highways in rural America can even be enlightening. I grew up working on my grandfather's farm, but never questioned a multitude of daily encounters with farm life.

For instance, why do cows chew their cud? For that matter, what is a cud? And, why do they spend so much time chewing it? Well, I got curious.

Cows first fill their stomachs with grass and other food. Then they settle down for a good, long, enjoyable chew. They bring the food back up from their stomachs and rework what they've already eaten, reexperiencing its goodness and transforming it into rich milk.

Chewing the cud—a process of meditating on turning alfalfa into body-building milk. Maybe it's not the most exciting thing you've learned this week, but it's fun and life-enriching to enlarge your understanding of life's most simple experiences.

A few additional topics have peaked my curiosity recently. Why do they lock the bathrooms in gas stations? I don't think anyone is going to break in and clean them. Why do we announce power outages on television? Is there another word for synonym? Why is the word "abbreviation" so long?

You'd be amazed how such curious thinking will allow you to expand your horizons.

In the end, it is important to remember that we cannot become what we need to be by remaining what we are.

MAX DEPREE

HOW INFORMED ARE YOU?

What's an expert? I read somewhere that the more a man knows, the more he knows he doesn't know. So I suppose one definition of an expert would be someone who doesn't admit outloud that he knows enough about a subject to know he doesn't really know much.

MALCOLM
FORBES

❀

P erhaps you read about the work of Professor Herb Dordick of the University of Southern California Annenberg School of Communications. Professor Dordick divides people into two categories: First are those who are "being informed" and the other group are those who are "getting informed."

The 10 percent of the population who are "getting informed" actively pursue new information. According to Professor Dordick, "Those 'being informed' are the ones inundated with information who have no strategy to separate the noise and clutter from that which is useful, valuable, and which fuels their innovation machine."

"Getting informed" and keeping informed produces knowledge that, when applied, generates substantial payoffs. Knowledge is the link between problems and solutions. It provides a bridge to cross from possibilities to inventions, from ideas to discoveries, from action to results.

Charlie Steinmetz was a well-informed electrical engineer. He knew his stuff. When Henry Ford experienced a break down in his electrical generators in Dearborn, Michigan, he knew the resulting stalled production line could produce disastrous results. Local electricians were unable to solve his problem, so Mr. Ford contacted his friend Charlie.

Steinmetz walked into the plant and surveyed the problem. He tinkered here and tinkered there. Ford's employees questioned his supposed electronic genius. In fact, they went to Henry Ford and exclaimed, "This guy doesn't know what he's doing. He just walks the plant and tinkers around." Ford assured them that Charlie knew what he was doing.

Charlie entered the plant the next morning to continue his tinkering. He walked over to the generators, flipped the switch, and machines began humming. Within a few minutes, everything was back to normal. The Ford employees stood in disbelief with their mouths hanging open.

Steinmetz sent Henry Ford a bill for $10,000. Ford responded, "Charlie, you're a great friend but isn't $10,000 a bit much for some tinkering around?"

Charlie immediately replied, "I'm only charging you $10 for tinkering around and $9,990 for *knowing where* to tinker."

The expression for learning in Chinese is made up of two symbols: One stands for studying, the other for practicing constantly. So, you cannot think of learning without thinking of practicing constantly.

PETER
SENGE

❊

We're all like Charlie Steinmetz. Our value is based on what we know and our ability to put what we know to use. Getting informed, being knowledgeable, and increasing our desire and ability to learn are of paramount importance in this vastly changing world. Without this lifestyle, we become a mere expense, a liability.

Robert Heller suggested in the *Super Manager* that you "Get to know what it is you don't know as fast as you can." If you want to avoid falling victim to changing conditions, equip yourself with more than a smattering of semi-useful information. Find out what you need to learn and unlearn to insure your survival.

Do you have the knowledge necessary to make informed decisions? Are you continually scrambling to understand the specific information required to take appropriate action and produce desired results? Do you have a passion to be the expert in your field? Are you taking advantage of situations that will advance your understanding and expertise? These are the collective abilities of people capable of remaining on the cutting edge.

The philosopher Goethe reflected, "All the knowledge I possess everyone else can acquire, but my heart is my own."

Information without the ambition to apply it is like a bird without wings. It's only a nicety incapable of producing what's necessary. Realize that the difference between people who grow and live life enthusiastically, and people who stagnate, is often their commitment to apply what they know.

This discussion isn't intended to suggest that you must know everything there is to know about everything. Theodore Roosevelt told the delightful story of a businessperson who had consulted an attorney for legal advice. Having coffee with a friend one day, he recounted the experience.

"Why did you spend your hard-earned money for a lawyer?" asked the friend. "The law books in his office contain every answer you could ever want. Why didn't you just read the right book and find out the answer for yourself? It would have saved you a lot of money."

"That's true," replied the businessperson, "but the difference is the lawyer knew what book and what page the answer was on."

I'm glad I can depend on other people's knowledge to assist me in some areas of my life. I can't repair a kitchen faucet, fix the brakes on my car, or do my own income tax. But I do hire people who know what they are doing and are considered the experts in their chosen fields. There's simply too much knowledge out there for me to learn in a lifetime. That's why it's so important for me to stay focused on the information I can apply in my specific arena. In this way, others can depend on me in my area of expertise.

We must dedicate ourselves to become lifelong learners. We must continually seek out resources and people willing to share their knowledge. There is no final graduation day for those who want to grow and prosper.

"That's all fine and dandy," you say. "But I don't have time for reading, listening, and attending seminars." Neither did John Wesley. But his passion for reading was so intense that he made it a part of his schedule. He read mostly on horseback. Wesley rode between 50 and 90 miles a day with a book propped up in his saddle . . . and got through thousands of volumes during his lifetime. Any more excuses? Become a sponge. Absorb and soak up everything you can.

"The older I get," said Abraham Lincoln, "the more I realize that there is but one wealth, one security on this earth and this is found in the ability of a person to perform a task well. And first and foremost, this ability must start with knowledge." Get informed!

IGNITE YOUR INNOVATIVE SPIRIT

The premier inventor Jerome Lemelson is responsible for such gizmos as Fax machines, VCRs, cordless phones, and cassette players. He is the fourth largest patent-holder in United States history and contributes his innovative success to continually finding problems to solve. He is also a prolific question asker. His favorite? "Is this the best way to do it? Is there a better way?"

Before Dick Fosbury appeared on the high-jump scene, the conventional way for high jumpers to cross the bar had been with a forward leap.

Fosbury introduced the world to a far different technique at the 1968 Olympics in Mexico City. He took four or five bounding strides and lifted himself off the ground. Then, in mid-air, he did something no Olympic athlete had ever done before. He turned his back to the bar and cleared it. With an Olympic record leap of 7 feet, 4-1/4 inches, his new "Fosbury Flop" became the standard. He found a better way by not imitating what others had done before.

Nothing limits achievement like small thinking; nothing expands possibilities like unleashed imagination.

WILLIAM ARTHUR WARD

Discontinue accepting everything as it is. We need to rethink and possibly reinvent everything we do. It is a matter of survival in our fast-paced, changing world. Question the rules, traditions, and conformity that block innovation. Begin asking, "What do we currently do that we could stop doing?" "What do we have that we don't need?" "What aren't we doing that we should start doing?" "What do we need that we don't have?"

"That all sounds fine," you say, "but I haven't been trained enough to pull this off." Some of the most successful entrepreneurs in our country knew nothing about the business they started. A host of famous artists couldn't draw. There are musicians who can't read music.

Remember the Beatles. They produced over 170 songs and took the global music scene by storm. At one time, their records accounted for a whopping 60 percent of all U.S. music sales. Here's the irony. John Lennon and Paul McCartney couldn't read or write music. Amazing. Don't think you can't create something of value just because you don't have the education or training to do it. In fact, you probably have a head start.

Learn to foster new ideas by placing yourself in learning situations. Genius blooms in originality. Experts tend to think in structured ways and thereby inhibit their ingenuity. Innovative thinking begins with forgetting or deliberately placing conventional thinking on the back burner. Unlearning what you've learned allows your mind to flow freely.

It might be a fun and beneficial experiment to approach the next week like the characters on the television series "3rd Rock from the Sun." Watch a few reruns. The writer certainly approaches earthlings' accepted way of doing things from the ridiculous viewpoint of space aliens. I like their naivety, willingness to question everything, and act as if they have no idea about what is normal.

Look at things through fresh eyes. Think like a beginner with no preconceived idea of how things should work, what things fit where, and how simple life tasks should be completed.

You'll be amazed at what an innovative expert you can become by acting like a beginner. You might also discover some wonderful things about yourself, your potential, and the world around you.

The guy who invented the first wheel was an idiot. The guy who invented the other three, he was a genius.

SID CAESAR

TAKE CHARGE OF YOUR FUTURE

Our limited perspective, our hopes and fears become our measure of life, and when circumstances don't fit our ideas, they become our difficulties.

BENJAMIN FRANKLIN

LIFE IS LIFE

I live under a simple set of operating principles that naturally contribute to ongoing positive mental health. What you are about to read is not profound, but it is important. *Life is life.*

Life is not good. Life is not bad. Life is life. It contains positive experiences as well as unwanted ones. Life awaits me fresh each day with possibilities and obstacles. At the conclusion of my day, I often reflect on the learning I've experienced and the periodic pain I needed to endure. Life is life.

At the core of being uptight with life is our unwillingness to accept life for what it is, even when it occurs different from our expectations. To maintain a healthy perspective, we would do well to understand Abraham Maslow's seven requirements for mental health:

1. Take responsibility for your own feelings, including your happiness. Never give ownership or control of your feelings to someone else. When you refuse to

True maturity only comes when you finally realize that no one is coming to the rescue.

AUTHOR
UNKNOWN

acknowledge the fact that your feelings are yours and no one else's, only *you* are deceived and injured.

2. Give up the luxury of blaming others for your shortcomings, disappointments, and suffering.

When you evaluate all of the good things that happen in your life, who is responsible? Now reflect on the shortcomings, disappointments, and suffering. Who caused them? How easy it is to take the credit for positive outcomes and pass off responsibility for what we don't like to someone else. How fair is that?

The day we stop making excuses and declare ourselves accountable is the day we can begin bringing closure and start dumping the emotional garbage of the past.

3. Face the consequences, even when the things you attempt and the risks you take bring about the worst possible results.

Two-time Pulitzer Prize winner Barbara Tuchman said, "Taking responsibility for your behavior, your expenditures and your actions and not forever supposing that society must forgive you because it's 'not your fault' is the quality most needed in [this] century."

4. Seek to discover all of the inner resources that are available to you, even though self-discovery is at times painful and demanding. It takes courage to unveil the true feelings we have of ourselves. When you recognize the talents you possess, values you endorse, and the attitudes that shape your life, you're in a position to focus on improving yourself and reaching your potential.

5. Act on your own feelings, rather than on the approval of others—even if this means conflict at times with those who are important to you. Thomas Jefferson once said, "In matters of taste, swim in the current; in matters of principle, stand like a rock." Flexibility, the ability to go with the flow, is an admirable personality trait unless it violates character. Compromised values will disintegrate your integrity. Act on your belief in what is right.

6. Take responsibility for letting go of your own negativity, including letting yourself and other people off the hook. That which we consistently think about expands. Letting go of negativity requires the disposing of negative input. Choose to fill the thoughts of your mind and emotions in your heart with that which builds you up.

Refuse to think about, dwell on, or be influenced by the mass of negative information fighting to saturate your life. Let it go! Also release the negative judgments of others that haunt your mind.

7. Have compassion and empathy for yourself and for others, recognizing that having compassion is a very healing process. Learn to be a nice person. Be respectful. Listen to people. Find out what's important to others. Uphold people's dignity. Add joy to their lives. Accept others for who they are. Give up criticizing. Be genuinely interested in the lives of other people. Life begins infinitely more positive when we have compassion and empathy for people.

Life is life. But it inevitably returns to us what we invest in it. Decide what you want from life and begin putting in what you're hoping to reap from life.

CHOOSE YOUR RESPONSE

Those adapting well to changing times have a change-less character that provides a foundation from which they make choices to deal effectively with a vastly changing world. A spirit of innovation and personal growth allows them to adapt, accept, and even embrace the changes around them without violating their personal principles.

We can't deny the nature of our changing culture or avoid it. Change unfolds unknown variables in our lives and plans. Resist the temptation to go about your daily business blind to the unpredictable. Just because you "keep doing what you're doing" does not necessarily mean you'll keep getting what you've been getting. Actually, denial and business as usual is bound to produce less than satisfying results.

There is a courthouse in Ohio that stands in a unique location. When it rains, the rain that falls on the north side of the roof drains into Lake Ontario and flows into the Gulf of St.

Too many people fear change. They cling to the familiar old shoe even if it cuts off circulation to their toes.

WALLY "FAMOUS" AMOS

Lawrence. Rain falling on the south side ends up in the Mississippi River and ultimately flows into the Gulf of Mexico.

The destiny of those raindrops can be altered by a gentle breeze or sudden gust of wind and will make a difference of more than 2,000 miles in their final destination. The raindrops don't have a choice in their final destination. You do.

You have at your disposal exactly what you need to gain confidence in dealing with the winds of change. The strongest principle for determining your ultimate destination lies in the choices you make.

You make two choices in response to life's events. First, you choose one course of action or mental response. By so doing, you are not choosing the opposite response. If you choose to proactively deal with circumstances, you are making a decision not to allow the circumstances to control you. You'll create internal resiliency and outward productivity.

Second, you must choose to give an honest effort to make that action or response a reality. This normally requires you to move out of your comfort zone into the unknown. That requires a willingness to risk discomfort, face challenges head on, and draw on your resources to make the best of every situation.

This is critical! As Gloria Estephan beautifully sings: "We seal our fate with the choices we make." We control the choices we make and then the choices control us.

It is important to invest our energies in things over which we have control versus no-control issues. Many people find it easier to focus on, worry about, and complain about things outside their control. Why? It doesn't take any effort. Many people don't want to act; they want to whine and fret. Action takes too much work.

Remember, you can't always control what happens to you in life. Sometimes you can, sometimes you can't. You can, however, always control how you look at and deal with what happens to you. You can control your blood pressure, your heart rate, the way you treat people, the commitment you have to your job, how many times you tell your children how much you love them, and a multitude of other things. You always have some control.

Abandon the energy you are throwing at uncontrollable events. It's a waste of time. Salute the reality of change and the fact that you can't control everything in your life. Get on with life by separating the controllable and uncontrollable events in your life, and invest your psychological

All of life is a series of choices, and what you choose to give life today will determine what life will give you tomorrow.

ZIG ZIGLAR

❋

energies in determining how you will deal with life's detours and opportunities.

We either choose to create the quality of each day or accept a life sentence of wallowing in tension, anger, stress, and discouragement. Refusing to make careful choices when change is all around you allows the events to shape and control your life. Unfortunately, you'll end up emotionally and physically exhausted.

Do you want to change the impact change has on your life? Then change the way you respond to it. As Jungian analyst and philosopher James Hillman has said: "Insanity is doing the same thing over and over again and expecting different results."

CREATE A CHOICE CREDO

I like life-enhancing principles that are simple to understand. Og Mandino's observation falls into that category. He identified a better way to live with just one word. Choice!

I've decided there are three basic things I need to remember about life:

1. **I cannot always control everything that happens to me.** Sometimes I can. Sometimes I can't.

2. **I can always control how I respond to any situation.** The attitudes, reactions, and perspectives I experience are my personal choice.

3. **Therefore, I always have some degree of control over my life.** Although the circumstances are often uncontrollable, I alone decide how I will respond.

This comprehensive approach has compelled me to create a "choice credo" for my life. It is a self-empowering way to

There is a better way to live. Choice! The key is choice. You have options. Those who live in unhappy failure have never exercised their options for a better way of life because they have never been aware that they had any choices!

OG MANDINO,
The Choice

remind me of the power I have to make choices and take action. This credo has allowed me to determine my level of dissatisfaction or satisfaction, frustration or contentment, happiness or grief. A warning light goes off when I waver from my commitment. I feel out of control and a sense of powerlessness sets in.

C. S. Lewis said, "Every time you make a choice you are turning the control part of you, the part that chooses, into something a little different from what it was before. And taking your life as a whole, with all your innumerable choices, you are slowly turning this control thing either into a heavenly creature or into a hellish one." Here is the personal credo of choice that helps to turn my relationships, life, and career into a "heavenly creature."

Choice Credo

I choose to be excited and enthusiastic about every minute of every day.

I choose to be energetic, productive, and sensitive to how I use my time by carefully determining my priorities.

I choose to apply my energies on solutions, answers, and options rather than becoming engulfed in problems.

I choose to positively affect the lives of people through nurturing, support, and encouragement.

I choose to control my attitude and strive to see the bright side.

I choose to develop the qualities and characteristics that will bring achievement, successful results, and personal fulfillment.

I choose to give every task my best effort and unrestricted energy.

I choose to carefully consider my response to difficult, critical, and controlling people.

I choose to be a caring, loving husband and father, determined to help my family live life to the fullest.

I choose to involve myself in activities that strengthen me physically, mentally, emotionally, and spiritually.

I certainly don't mean to imply I've mastered or perfected my "choice credo." It's a daily challenge to live up to the standards expressed; but by striving to accept responsibility for my life choices, actions, and attitudes, I'm giving myself permission to determine the quality of my life. When I make wise deci-

In the long run, we shape our lives and we shape ourselves. The process never ends until we die. And the choices we make are ultimately our own responsibility.

ELEANOR
ROOSEVELT

✺

sions, I reap positive results. When I choose to become a victim of past experiences, present circumstances, or other people, the hope for a better life is deflated.

Don't become a victim of yourself. Determine what is working in your life and what isn't. Is what you're doing today advancing you toward what you want to be tomorrow? Don't go through the day with your fingers crossed, saying, "I hope things get better soon." Make choices based upon your values, rather than circumstances or feelings. Do what is right regardless of how you feel. The feelings will follow.

Arnold J. Toynbee said, "As human beings, we are endowed with freedom of choice, and we cannot shuffle off our responsibility upon the shoulders of God or nature. We must shoulder it ourselves. It is up to us." Choose to become all you can be by committing yourself to your own "choice credo."

INSIST ON INTERNAL ACCOUNTABILITY

The ability to enjoy the future rests with us and not a dependence on other people to get us through. Accountability becomes a reality when you finally realize that no one is coming to the rescue. The starting point of personal accountability is for you to accept complete responsibility for who you are and for everything that you become.

Here's a hint that will jump-start your life. *Realize that no one is coming to your rescue.* The degree to which you effectively deal with change is in direct proportion to the degree you feel you are in control of your life.

Victims produce self-imposed stress. They are preoccupied with the past and uncontrollable experiences filling their life with should-haves, could-haves, and would-haves. Victims go through the day with their fingers crossed, hoping things will get better; but they are convinced nothing they do will change their condition. Victims see themselves controlled by

My philosophy is that not only are you responsible for your life, but doing the best at this moment puts you in the best place for the next moment.

OPRAH
WINFREY

external circumstances. They put other people in charge of their moods. It's a no-win lifestyle created by a loser mindset.

Your attitude toward personal accountability is one of the most important statements you make about the kind of person you are and the degree of control you exhibit in your life. Taking responsibility for future results sows the seeds of positive emotions. It's great to have people around you to encourage, support, express appreciation, and offer assistance; but becoming dependent on others breeds disappointment and turns change into a threat. The old saying "If it is to be, it is up to me" serves us well here.

Competency, security, job satisfaction, personal fulfillment, and emotional health are an inside job. Nobody has been assigned to your case to insure your successful journey through present and future passages. "I am responsible." Say it to yourself. Accept it as a reality and mandatory course of study and mastery throughout the rest of your life.

No doubt about it; change is a learning experience. As Mark Twain observed, "A man who holds a cat by the tail learns something he can learn in no other way." You're right, Mr. Twain, and change also forces us to look at life's changing menu with maturing perspective.

Courageously face life with its uncertainties. There is a world full of opportunities waiting to be seized. Shedding old skin may involve pain, tears, sweat, and failure; but it clears your vision and becomes the motivation to capture your dreams.

Live in such a way that you would not be ashamed to sell your parrot to the town gossip.

WILL ROGERS

Glenn Van Ekeren is the Executive Vice President for Vetter Health Services in Omaha, Nebraska, a company committed to providing "dignity in life" for the elderly. As a professional speaker, he is known for his inspiring, enthusiastic, and down-to-earth approach for maximizing people and organizational potential. He is the author of a number of books, including *12 Simple Secrets of Happiness*; *Finding Joy in Everyday Relationships*, *12 Simple Secrets of Happiness at Work*; and *Speaker's Sourcebook I* and *II*.

For further information about Glenn Van Ekeren's seminars and other products, contact:

Glenn Van Ekeren
21134 Arbor Court
Elkhorn, Nebraska 68022
402-289-4523